Paperback Books for Children

*Compiled by the Committee on Paperback Lists
for Elementary Schools*

AMERICAN ASSOCIATION OF SCHOOL LIBRARIANS

*American Library Association,
Beatrice Simmons, Editor.*

CITATION PRESS

NEW YORK

1972

Published by Citation Press, Library and
Trade Division, Scholastic Magazines, Inc.,
Editorial Office: 50 West 44th Street,
New York, New York 10036

Library of Congress Catalog Card Number: 72-76489

Standard Book Number: 590-09542-0

Printed In the U. S. A.

010.52
A5125p

CONTENTS

PREFACE

Paperback Books for Children is a result of one of the activities of the Committee on Paperback Lists for Elementary Schools of the American Association of School Librarians. This compilation of nearly 700 titles was prepared by an ad hoc committee whose members were selected because they represent diversified backgrounds and broad experience in working with children and teachers in elementary schools.

The paperback books included in this list are, for the most part, those that have received favorable recommendation and high praise as hardbound books from one or more review and selection aids. Titles include those available through spring 1971. The books in this bibliography have been personally reviewed by the committee members or by other librarians and teachers.

The same criteria of content for selection used in choosing hardcover books for children was used in preparing this list of paperbacks. It is understood that paperback books do not meet the same format criteria used in selecting regular trade or library bound editions. A particular effort was made to choose books that will meet the curricular and recreational needs of today's child. In addition, other titles were included because they reflected a wide range of interests and a variety of scope and content necessary for enriching reading experiences. Some publications have been included that will be of particular value to the teacher and the librarian.

This list is intended as a guide for librarians and teachers who are interested in starting a paperback collection, supplementing an existing one, or purchasing multiple copies for classroom and library use. It will guide in the selection and assist in the purchase by identifying what paperbacks are available and where they can be obtained. Annotations are provided for each title listed, and information is given concerning publisher, imprint, and price. The suggested grade level of each book is also given. If no level is indicated, the book is suggested for teacher and advanced student use.

Frances Hatfield, PRESIDENT 1971–72
AMERICAN ASSOCIATION OF SCHOOL LIBRARIANS

SELECTION CRITERIA

The selection aids most generally used by elementary school librarians are: *Children's Catalog, Books for Elementary School Libraries, The Elementary School Library Collection, School Library Journal, The Booklist,* and *Horn Book.* Since librarians and teachers of children's literature rely on these sources in selecting hardcover books, they were equally useful as backlists from which to compile this paperback list. A title recommended in any of these selection aids was included providing the print was clear and readable, original illustrations or suitable alternates were used, and the work was essentially the same as the original. Thus all the books were personally reviewed by committee members or by librarians and teachers with whom they are associated.

The committee and their associates also personally reviewed titles not found in the selection aids and included those determined to be of potential interest to elementary school children because of their content, vocabulary, timeliness, and when they were written by authors who are authorities in their field.

PICTURE BOOKS

AUSTIN, MARGOT *Barney's Adventure* Illus. by the author.
Scholastic, 60¢ (K–2)
Barney follows some large footsteps into the woods hoping to get free tickets to the circus by capturing an escaped animal.

BEMELMANS, LUDWIG *Madeline* Illus. by the author.
Viking (Seafarer), 95¢ (K–3)
Twelve girls in a girls' school but only Madeline, the littlest, has the distinction of having her appendix out. In verse.

BEMELMANS, LUDWIG, *Madeline's Rescue* Illus. by the author.
Scholastic (Starline), 75¢ (K–3)
Sharing the puppy who saved Madeline from drowning causes a problem at the girls' school. Awarded the Caldecott Medal in 1954.

BISHOP, CLAIRE. *The Five Chinese Brothers.* Illus. by Kurt Wiese.
Scholastic, 60¢ (K–2)
The five Chinese brothers take advantage of their likenesses and their remarkable individual characteristics to save one of the brothers from having his head cut off.

BONSALL, CROSBY NEWELL *The Case of the Hungry Stranger* Illus. by the author.
Scholastic, 60¢ (1–2)
Who ate Mrs. Mesch's blueberry pie? Wizard, the private eye, and his friends track down the culprit. An I Can Read mystery.

Bridwell, Norman *Clifford Gets a Job* Illus. by the author.
Scholastic, 50¢ (1–2)
Clifford, a big red dog, becomes a wage earner with disastrous and hilarious results.

Bridwell, Norman *Clifford Takes a Trip* Illus. by the author.
Scholastic (Starline), 50¢ (1–2)
When the family goes on vacation, Clifford, their large red dog, becomes so lonely that he sets out to find his people. This trip has uproarious consequences!

Bridwell, Norman *A Tiny Family* Illus. by the author.
Scholastic, 50¢ (K–2)
A family of imaginative tiny people has many amusing problems in the real world of normal-size folks.

Bridwell, Norman *What Do They Do When It Rains?* Illus. by the author.
Scholastic, 50¢ (K–3)
This simple picture book suggest some amusing ways for people who work outdoors to use their talents when it rains.

Bridwell, Norman *The Witch's Christmas* Illus. by the author.
Scholastic 50¢ (K–2)
A friendly neighborhood witch livens up usual Christmas activities for a little girl and her brother.

Bright, Robert *Georgie* Illus. by the author.
Scholastic, 60¢ (K–3)
Georgie, a ghost, is forced to leave the house he always haunted and is unable to find another because each house already has a ghost.

Brown, Margaret Wise *Where Have You Been?* Illus. by Barbara Cooney.
Scholastic, 50¢ (K–2)
Every young child's fancy is sure to be captured by these charming, simple verses about familiar birds and animals.

Cameron, Polly *I Can't Said the Ant!* Illus. by the author.
Scholastic, 60¢ (K–2)
The teapot falls, but the ant alone can't lift her back onto the shelf.

Chance, E. B. *Just in Time for the King's Birthday* Illus. by Arline Meyer.
Scholastic, 50¢ (1–2)
A farmer makes a cheese for the king's birthday but encounters so

many hungry animals on his way to the palace that he ends up
with nothing for the king.

CARROLL, RUTH *What Whiskers Did* Illus. by the author.
Scholastic, 60¢ (K–1)
In this complete picture book, no words are used, or necessary, to
show what Whiskers does when he runs away and chases a rabbit.

CHARLIP, REMY *Where is Everybody?* Illus. by the author.
Scholastic, 60¢ (1–2)
This is an artfully constructed book, with simple line drawings and
very brief text, describing a sunny scene and what happens to
people, animals, and birds when a rain storm came up.

CRAIG, JEAN M. *The New Boy on the Sidewalk* Illus. by Sheila
Greenwald.
Young Readers, 60¢ (K–3)
Dislike turns into trust when the need for protection from older
boys on the block cause the new boy and the old boy to join forces.

DAUGHERTY, JAMES *Andy and the Lion* Illus. by the author.
Viking (Seafarer), 75¢ (K–3)
Modern version of Androcles and the lion.

DENNIS, WESLEY *Flip* Illus. by the author.
Viking (Seafarer), 85¢ (K–3)
Flip can't jump across the brook, until he dreams he has wings and
doesn't realize it's only a dream.

DENNIS, WESLEY *Flip and the Morning* Illus. by the author.
Viking (Seafarer), 65¢ (K–3)
Flips's early rising disturbs the whole barnyard until Willie, the
goat, tells him to hunt for the wise old wood duck who lives in a
spring that can only be located in the early morning.

ELKIN, BENJAMIN *Lucky and the Giant* Illus. by Brinton Turkle.
Scholastic, 50¢ (K–2)
Lucky, with luck and a bit of cleverness, rescues his parents from
bondage to the giant.

ELKIN, BENJAMIN *Six Foolish Fishermen* Illus. by Bernice Myers.
Scholastic, 50¢ (K–1)
Six brothers who have gone fishing count themselves at the end of
the day and discover they've lost one. Based on an old folktale.

EMBERLEY, BARBARA, ADAPTER *One Wide River to Cross* Illus. by
Edward Emberley.
> Scholastic (Starline), 75¢ (1–3)

A counting book set to the tune of an old folk song about the
animals entering Noah's ark.

ETS, MARIE HALL *Gilberto and the Wind* Illus. by the author.
> Viking (Seafarer), 85¢ (1–3)

Beautiful illustrations and easy-to-read text describe the adventures of a little Spanish boy and his friend, the wind.

ETS, MARIE HALL *In the Forest* Illus. by the author.
> Viking (Seafarer), 75¢ (K–1)

A boy's walk in the forest turns into a parade of wild animals and a
party until the appearance of the boy's father makes them disappear.

ETS, MARIE HALL *Just Me* Illus. by the author.
> Viking (Seafarer), 75¢ (K–1)

The little boy telling the story can walk like a cat, a cow, and a
horse, and imitate other animals too, until he has to run to catch
Dad in time to take a boat ride.

ETS, MARIE HALL *Play With Me* Illus. by the author.
> Viking (Seafarer), 75¢ (K–1)

A little girl, looking for a playmate, tries to catch several woodland
animals, but they all run away until she sits quietly and let them
come to her.

ETS, MARIE HALL *Talking Without Words* Illus. by the author.
> Viking (Seafarer), 75¢ (K–1)

This enjoyable little book tells that often "actions speak louder
than words" and shows a child how he can communicate without
speaking.

FATIO, LOUISE *The Happy Lion* Illus. by Roger Duvoisin.
> Scholastic, 75¢ (K–3)

The happy lion finds that the friends who visit him in the zoo
behave very differently when he escapes from the zoo and goes to
visit them.

FREEMAN, DON *Corduroy* Illus. by the author.
> Viking (Seafarer), 95¢ (K–2)

Delightful pictures and text tell the story of a lonely little
stuffed bear who finally finds a small black girl to love and care
for him.

FREEMAN, DON   *Dandelion*   Illus. by the author.
Viking (Seafarer), 65¢   (K–3)
"I will never again try to turn myself into a stylish dandy. From
now on I'll always be just plain me," vows Dandelion, the lion,
when he almost misses Jennifer Giraffe's party because she didn't
recognize the silly looking lion who came to the door.

FREEMAN, DON   *Mop Top*   Illus. by the author.
Viking (Seafarer), 95¢   (K–1)
"This is the story of a boy who never wanted to have his hair cut"
until, while he was hiding from the barber, a woman mistakes his
head for a fluffy mop.

FREEMAN, DON   *Norman the Doorman*   Illus. by the author.
Viking (Seafarer), 75¢   (K–3)
Norman, a mouse, is a doorman and a sculptor who lives in a
mouse hole in back of an art museum. It is there he created his
first sculpture that brought him first prize in an art contest. The
book boasts whimsical illustrations that should prove pleasing to
all readers.

FRISKEY, MARGARET   *Indian Two Feet and His Horse*   Illus. by Ezra
Jack Keats
Scholastic (Starline), 50¢   (K–2)
Indian Two Feet has to walk, because he has no horse. And when
he does find one, it has sore feet.

GALDONE, PAUL   *The Three Little Pigs*   Illus. by the author.
Scholastic, 75¢   (2–3)
This familiar tale of the three little pigs and their struggles with
the villianous wolf comes to life with colorful full-page illustrations.

GRAHAM, AL   *Timothy Turtle*   illus. by Tony Palazzo.
Viking (Seafarer), 75¢   (K–3)
Timothy, the traveling turtle, sets out for fun and frolic and
encounters joy and some sadness on his adventuresome trail.
Drawings enhance the verse with humor and information.

HADER, BERTA   *The Mighty Hunter*   Illus. by Berta and Elmer
Hader.
Scholastic 60¢   (K–3)
It is more fun to go hunting than to go to school, so Little Brave
Heart aims at a wood rat, who leads him on to larger game and
eventually to a bear who hunts only when hungry.

HEIDE, FLORENCE PARRY, AND VAN CLIEF, SYLVIA WORTH *That's What Friends Are For* Illus. by Brinton Turkle.

Scholastic, 75¢ (1–3)

Theodore, an elephant, receives much advice from his friends until one friend says that friends are to help—so they do.

HOBAN, RUSSELL *Charlie the Tramp* Illus. by Lillian Hoban.

Scholastic, 60¢ (1–3)

Charlie, a beaver, decides that being a beaver is too hard work; he'd rather be a tramp. But strangely, the tramp turns into a beaver.

HOBAN, RUSSELL *Nothing To Do* Illus. by Lillian Hoban.

Scholastic (Starline), 60¢ (1–3)

When Walter Possum's father gives him a magic stone, he no longer has the problem of finding something to do.

HOFF, SYD *The Witch, the Cat, and the Baseball Bat* Illus. by the author.

Young Readers, 60¢ (K–3)

There was once a witch who disliked baseball tremendously. She stays up late one night to plan a way to ruin baseball and make the spectators uninterested in the game. Her pixie plans produce some hilarious happenings.

IVIMEY, JOHN W. *The Adventures of the Three Blind Mice* Illus. by Nola Langner.

Scholastic (Starline), 50¢ (1–3)

The words and music of the song are also given. The story tells how the mice became blind, why their tails were cut off, and how they recovered.

JOHNSON, CROCKETT *A Picture for Harold's Room* Illus. by the author.

Scholastic (Starline), 60¢ (K–2)

Harold takes his purple crayon to draw a picture for his room. As usual, things get a little out-of-hand, but he manages to save himself. A Purple Crayon Adventure.

JOSLIN, SESYLE *What Do You Say, Dear?* Illus. by Maurice Sendak.

Scholastic, 60¢ (K–3)

The polite usages are the correct answers to ridiculous situations, such as what do you say to Bad-Nose Bill who asks, "Would you like me to shoot a hole in your head?" The answer, "No, thank you."

JULIAN, NANCY R.   *The Peculiar Miss Pickett*   Illus. by Donald E. Cooke.

Scholastic, 50¢   (3–5)

Miss Pickett is a wonderful but strange babysitter. Magical, exciting things happen to Carol and Bobby everytime she comes to stay with them.

KEATS, EZRA JACK   *The Snowy Day*   Illus. by the author.

Scholastic, 75¢   (K–2)

Want some ideas of what to play in the snow? Awarded the Caldecott Medal in 1963.

KENT, JACK   *Just Only John*   Illus. by the author.

Grosset Young Readers, 60¢   (K–3)

John, a little boy of four, was bored with his life and decided to buy a new one. The problems he encounters help him to grow up.

KOHLER, JULILLY H.   *The Boy Who Stole the Elephant*   Illus. by Lee Ames.

Scholastic, 50¢   (4–6)

Queenie, the elephant, makes the little circus a smashing success and brings happiness to Gyp who works there. But the evil plans of the circus owner prompt Gyp to take Queenie away and set the scene for adventures of boy and elephant.

KRASILOVSKY, PHYLLIS   *The Cow Who Fell in the Canal*   Illus. by Peter Spier.

Scholastic, 75¢   (1–3)

Hendrika is unhappy with her life on a Holland farm and longs to see the city. How she finally gets to the city and her adventures there are highlighted by colorful, full-page pictures.

KRASILOVSKY, PHYLLIS   *The Man Who Didn't Wash His Dishes*   Illus. by Barbara Cooney.

Scholastic, 50¢   (K–3)

Believe it or not, you can go without washing dishes after your meals only so long; even if you're willing to eat from soap dishes, ash trays, and flower pots.

KRAUSS, RUTH   *Bears*   Illus. by Phyllis Rowand.

Scholastic, 50¢   (K–2)

All the kinds of bears—in rhyme. Text consists of only 17 words.

KRAUSS, RUTH   *The Carrot Seed*   Illus. by Crockett Johnson.

Scholastic, 50¢   (K–1)

The moral of this story is you have to have faith, and you don't have to believe everything older folks tell you. After all, you're the one who planted the carrot seed.

KRAUSS, RUTH   *The Happy Egg*   Illus. by Crockett Johnson.
Scholastic, 50¢   (K–2)
Once there was a little bird who was still just an egg and could do nothing but be sat on and sat on. Then, pop, the little bird could do everything, even grow up and sit on other happy eggs.

KRAUSS, RUTH   *Is This You?*   Illus. by Crockett Johnson.
Scholastic, 60¢   (K–1)
A fun-filled picture book that asks the child questions about himself and encourages him to draw his answers.

LEAF, MUNRO   *The Boy Who Would Not Go to School*   Illus. by the author.
Scholastic (Starline), 60¢   (K–1)
Robert Francis refuses to go to school until he is grown up. Each year he grows bigger, but there is nothing Robert Francis can do because he will not go to school. Finally he gives in and Robert Francis has a good time. Originally titled *Robert Francis Weatherbee*.

LEAF, MUNRO   *Gordon, the Goat*   Illus. by the author.
Scholastic (Starline), 60¢   (1–2)
Gordon decides not to be like all the other goats and follow the leader. This decision is reached only after Gordon is led into a "twister" and was whirled around.

LEAF, MUNRO   *The Story of Ferdinand*   Illus. by Robert Lawson.
Viking (Seafarer), 75¢   (K–2)
Who wants to fight when you can sit and smell flowers? Ferdinand the bull was the first of the flower children.

LEXAU, JOAN   *Olaf Reads*   Illus. by Harvey Weiss.
Scholastic, 60¢   (1–2)
After some interesting experiences, Olaf realizes that he must not only learn to read, but he must learn to think about what he reads.

LIONNI, LEO   *Inch by Inch*   Illus. by the author.
Scholastic, 75¢   (1–3)
Bold, colorful full-page illustrations dominate the story of a tiny inchworm and the birds he measures in exchange for not getting eaten.

LOW, JOSEPH *There Was a Wise Crow* Illus. by the author.
Scholastic, 75¢ (K–2)
This book of rhymed nonsense verses team up with adorable color illustrations to make for an enjoyable reading experience.

McCLOSKEY, ROBERT *Lentil* Illus. by the author.
Scholastic, 75¢ (2–4)
Old Sneep sucks a lemon to dry up the mouths of the band members when Colonel Carter comes to town. Lentil saves the day with his harmonica.

MERRIAM, EVE *Do You Want to See Something?* Illus. by Abner Graboff.
Scholastic, 50¢ (K–2)
This is an artfully constructed book, with simple line drawings that present engaging riddles for small children.

MOORE, LILIAN *Little Raccoon and the Outside World* Illus. by Gioia Fiammenghi.
Scholastic, 50¢ (1–2)
Little Raccoon leaves the forest and investigates a teeter-totter, a clothesline, a shower, and spaghetti.

NÖDSET, JOAN L. *Who Took the Farmer's Hat?* Illus. by Fritz Siebel.
Scholastic, 75¢ (K–1)
None of the farm animals have seen the farmer's hat. They have seen only a big round mousehole or a flower pot or a boat, but the bird has found a nest.

Old MacDonald Had a Farm Illus. by Abner Graboff.
Scholastic, 50¢ (K–2)
Bright, colorful pictures illustrate the words of the familiar song for children.

PARISH, PEGGY *Amelia Bedelia* Illus. by Fritz Siebel.
Scholastic, 50¢ (K–3)
A lemon meringue pie saves Amelia Bedelia's job after she takes her instructions too literally and puts powder on the furniture to dust it, airs the light bulbs to put them out, and so on.

PETERSON, JOHN *The Littles* Illus. by Roberta Carter Clark.
Scholastic, 60¢ (2–4)
The Littles are tiny people who live within the walls of the Biggs's

house. Their greatest fear, of course, is the mice. Thereupon hangs a tale.

PETERSON, JOHN   *The Littles Have a Wedding*   Illus. by Roberta Carter Clark.

Scholastic, 60¢   (3-4)

This tiny family, whose members are about as tall as a pencil, have quite an adventure preparing for their cousin's wedding.

PETERSON, JOHN   *The Littles Take a Trip*   Illus. by Roberta Carter Clark.

Scholastic, 60¢   (2-3)

The tiny family of Littles go on a surprising, sometimes terrifying, journey.

REY, H. A.   *Curious George*   Illus. by the author.

Scholastic, 75¢   (K-2)

George, a curious monkey, is captured in Africa by the Man in the Yellow Hat and brought to America. He turns in a fire alarm, escapes from jail, and takes a balloon flight.

REY, H. A.   *Curious George Gets a Medal*   Illus. by the author.

Scholastic, 75¢   (K-2)

It all starts when George tries to fill a fountain pen with a funnel. The story moves on to the museum and ends in a space ship.

REY, H. A.   *Curious George Rides a Bike*   Illus. by the author.

Scholastic, 75¢   (K-2)

This adventure moves fast. George "borrows" a bike, is picked up by an animal show, and saves a baby bear.

REY, H. A.   *Curious George Takes a Job*   Illus. by the author.

Scholastic, 75¢   (K-2)

George's jobs include dishwasher (with four hands), window washer, painter, and movie star.

REY, MARGARET, AND REY, H. A.   *Curious George Goes to the Hospital*   Illus. by H. A. Rey.

Scholastic, 75¢   (K-2)

George goes to the hospital to have a piece of jigsaw puzzle he swallowed removed. While there, his curiosity leads him into such amusing situations that he is good therapy for some of the other patients.

Robinson, Tom *Buttons* Illus. by Peggy Bacon.
Viking (Seafarer), 65¢ (2–3)
Buttons, an alley cat, has many rough times and hair-raising experiences before he becomes a gentleman.

Sauer, Julia L. *Mike's House* Illus. by Don Freeman.
Viking (Seafarer), 75¢ (K–3)
The happiest moments in Mike's week are his days at the public library. On one such day a very unexpected and exciting experience occurs that adds even more zeal to this special event in the week.

Sawyer, Ruth *Journey Cake, Ho!* Illus. by Robert McCloskey.
Viking (Seafarer), 75¢ (1–3)
Prose and poetry tell a whimsical tale of a rolling cake that comes to life and attracts the attention of all it passes by.

Schulz, Charles, M. *Happiness Is a Warm Puppy* Illus. by the author.
Scholastic, 75¢ (1 up)
The beloved *Peanuts* characters talk about happiness and what it means to different people.

Sendak, Maurice *Chicken Soup with Rice: A Book of Months* Illus. by the author.
Scholastic, 75¢ (K–1)
All seasons of the year are nice for eating chicken soup with rice.

Sendak, Maurice *Where the Wild Things Are* Illus. by the author.
Scholastic, 95¢ (2–4)
A small boy dreams about fantastic beasts in a jungle where he becomes king. Awarded the Caldecott Medal in 1964.

Singer, Susan *Kenny's Monkey* Illus. by Harvey Weiss.
Scholastic (Starline), 50¢ (1–2)
Kenny has an irrepressible monkey who can do anything that Kenny and his friends can—except read.

Slobodkina, Esphyr *Caps for Sale* Illus. by the author.
Scholastic, 60¢ (K–2)
Playful monkeys steal the peddler's entire supply of caps, but he cleverly figures out a way to get them back.

Softly, Barbara *Ponder and William* Illus. by Diana John.
Penguin (Puffin), 95¢ (K–2)
Ponder, an extraordinary panda, shares many exciting adventures with his friend William.

Thompson, Vivian L. *Sad Day, Glad Day* Illus. by Lilian Obligado.
Scholastic (Starline), 50¢ (1–3)
It's a sad day when you have to move and leave old friends and beloved places behind. It's a glad day when you make new friends.

Tripp, Edward *The Tin Fiddle* Illus. by Maurice Sendak.
Scholastic, 60¢ (K–2)
The tin fiddle sounded beautiful to Cicero as he played it but eventually he realizes that no one else—not his family nor any of the domestic or woods animals—liked it so he gives it to the mice for a new home.

Udry, Janice May *Let's Be Enemies* Illus. by Maurice Sendak.
Scholastic, 75¢ (K–1)
John works himself up into a temper over James's always wanting to be boss. A squabble develops between the boys, and they decide to be enemies. A moment later the crisis is past. Told by John.

Udry, Janice May *What Mary Jo Shared* Illus. by Eleanor Mill.
Scholastic (Starline), 60¢ (K–2)
Mary Jo is too shy to share anything at "show and tell" time. When she does have something, someone else has something better—until she brings her father. Only the pictures indicate that Mary Jo is black and attending an integrated school.

Udry, Janice May *What Mary Jo Wanted* Illus. by Eleanor Mill.
Young Readers, 75¢ (1–3)
Mary Jo's desire to own a pet causes minor disturbances in the house, but they are patiently and skillfully solved through Mary Jo's love for her puppy. Excellent book for teaching the care of pets.

Ungerer, Tomi *Crictor* Illus. by the author.
Scholastic (Starline), 60¢ (K–2)
Mme. Bodot receives a boa constrictor as a pet and adapts to him perfectly. Crictor aids the children at school and foils a burglary.

Waber, Bernard *Rich Cat, Poor Cat* Illus. by the author.
Scholastic, 95¢ (K–2)
The ways of life of a rich cat and of Scat, a poor cat alternate.

"Most cats are somebody's cat. Scat is nobody's cat" until the end of the book.

WARD, LYND   *The Biggest Bear*   Illus. by the author.

Scholastic, 60¢   (K–3)

Attempting to get a bearskin such as the neighbors have for the barndoor, Johnny comes home with a baby bear that grows into the biggest bear around and causes the biggest problems. Awarded the Caldecott Medal in 1953.

WOODS, BETTY   *My Box and String*   Illus. by the author.

Scholastic, 50¢   (K–1)

The little boy is so selfish that he has to spend all his time guarding his boxes to keep away the people and animals who want to share them. In verse.

YASHIMA, TARO   *Crow Boy*   Illus. by the author.

Viking (Seafarer), 95¢   (1–3)

Chibi's classmates believe he is slow and stupid until they learn of his secret talent, which prompts them to nickname him "Crow Boy." Beautiful, full-page pictures help tell the story.

YASHIMA, TARO   *Umbrella*   Illus. by the author.

Viking (Seafarer), 75¢   (K–3)

Momo, which means "the peach" in Japanese, waits not so patiently for the day she can wear her birthday present—shiny red boots and an umbrella—and finally experiences the mystical qualities of a rain storm.

ZION, GENE   *No Roses for Harry!*   Illus. by Margaret Bloy Graham.

Scholastic, 60¢   (K–2)

Harry, a dog, is ashamed of his sweater that has roses on it, but he can't get rid of it for fear of hurting Grandma's feelings.

ZOLOTOW, CHARLOTTE   *Mr. Rabbit and the Lovely Present*   Illus. by Maurice Sendak.

Scholastic (Starline), 75¢   (K–2)

All the different colors are discussed as Mr. Rabbit and the little girl choose a present for the little girl's mother.

FICTION

ACKER, HELEN   *The School Train*   Illus. by Mort Kunstler.

Scholastic, 60¢   (3–5)

Tony, age 11, and John, age 9, can shoot and skin a squirrel and build and maintain an outdoor fire overnight, but they have never seen a book nor heard a radio. By themselves they travel 20 miles through the Canadian forest in winter to the place where the government school train is stationed temporarily so they can learn to read.

AIKEN, JOAN   *Nightbirds on Nantucket*   Illus. by Robin Jacques.

Dell (Yearling), 75¢   (5–7)

A pink whale and a Hanoverian plot to overthrow King James III are among the fanciful ingredients in this delightful tale in which London-born Dido Twite saves the island of Nantucket from destruction.

AIKEN, JOAN   *The Wolves of Willoughby Chase*   Illus. by Pat Marriott.

Dell (Yearling), 75¢   (5–7)

Independent Bonnie and her shy cousin Sylvia battle the perils of wolves roaming the countryside, an evil governess left to take care of them, and cruel imprisonment in an orphanage as they try to regain Bonnie's inheritance.

ALCOTT, LOUISA MAY   *Little Men*

Airmont, 95¢; Macmillan (Collier), 95¢   (5–7)

This novel reading experience for modern youth alternates between ideas for pranks they can pull and huge doses of old-fashioned manners and courtesy with a good deal of moralizing, but no real plot.

ALCOTT, LOUISA MAY *Little Women*
                    Airmont, 95¢; Macmillan (Collier) 95¢;
         Penguin (Puffin), 95¢; Scholastic (Starline), 75¢ (5–8)
Despite the occasional sermonettes, this story of how the four March girls with their individual personalities meet the problems of poverty, romance, and tragedy in their lives is still a winner.

ALEXANDER, LLOYD *The Black Cauldron*
                    Dell (Yearling), 75¢ (5–7)
The chronicle of Prydain continues as Taran, assistant pigkeeper, and his friends set out to destroy the Black Cauldron of Arawn, the lord of the Land of Death.

ALEXANDER, LLOYD *The Book of Three*
                    Dell (Yearling), 75¢ (5–7)
An introduction to the land of Prydain, born in Welsh mythology but turned into fantasy. Characters include an oracular pig and his keeper, a lord whose harp strings break when he elaborates on the truth, Gurgi—half animal and half man—a dwarf who can't disappear, and royalty galore.

ALEXANDER, LLOYD *The High King*
                    Dell (Yearling), 95¢ (5–7)
In the conclusion of the series, the forces of good gather for the final battle against the death lord. Allies change sides, and questions are answered. Awarded the Newbery Medal in 1969.

ANCKARSVARD, KARIN *The Mysterious Schoolmaster* Illus. by Paul Galdone.
                    Harcourt (Voyager), 75¢ (4–6)
Michael and Cecilia puzzle over the strange behavior of the new physics teacher and a mechanic with a foreign accent in a combination of school story and mystery. Translated from the Swedish.

ANCKARSVARD, KARIN *Rider by Night* Illus. by Charles W. Walker.
                    Scholastic, 75¢ (4–6)
Jenny lives and breathes to ride her horse Rascal. But joy turns into anxiety when she discovers a mysterious person is riding her beloved horse at night. Included in the story is an interesting description of Saint Lucia Day, a Swedish Christmas celebration. Translated from the Swedish by Annabelle Macmillan.

ANCKARSVARD, KARIN *The Robber Ghost*
                                    Harcourt (Voyager), 75¢ (4–6)
A new boy in school, a ghost in the castle, and a robbery from the
post office give Michael and Cecilia several mysteries to solve.
Translated from the Swedish.

ANDERSON, CLARENCE W. *Afraid to Ride* Illus. by the author.
                                    Scholastic, 60¢ (4–6)
"A bad horse took it away and maybe a good horse will give it
back," Mr. Jeffers said about Judy's love of riding, and he was
right.

ASHLEY, ROBERT *The Stolen Train* Illus. by Albert Micale.
                                    Scholastic, 75¢ (4–6)
Based on a true incident, this exciting Civil War story relates the
daring attempts of a small group of Union soldiers to steal a
Confederate train and run it to Chattanooga on an important
mission.

ATWATER, RICHARD, AND ATWATER, FLORENCE *Mr. Popper's Penguins* Illus. by Robert Lawson.
                                    Scholastic, 60¢ (4–6)
A gift of one penguin radically changes life in the Popper household as the one increases to twelve penguins and a new job.

BAGNOLD, ENID *National Velvet*
                                    Scholastic, 60¢ (4–6)
The story of the butcher's daughter who illegally, as a female,
races a piebald in the Grand National and unbelievably wins is
merely the climax of a warm English family story.

BAILEY, CAROLYN SHERWIN *Miss Hickory* Illus. by R. Gannett.
                                    Viking (Seafarer), 85¢ (4–6)
Hardheadedness, even if caused by one's head's being a hickory
nut, can make one miss out on a lot. Miss Hickory, the country doll,
makes this discovery as she resists the changes forced upon her by
having to live outdoors on her own. Awarded the Newbery Medal
in 1947.

BALL, ZACHARY *Bristle Face*
                                    Scholastic (Starline), 60¢ (4–6)
A dog who "started out to be a hound, then decided he'd look better
as a porcupine" befriends runaway orphan Jase Landers, aids a
romance, and becomes the top foxhound of the area—an honor
that eventually results in his death.

BARNOUW, VICTOR   *Dream of the Blue Heron*   Illus. by Lynd Ward.
Dell (Yearling), 75¢   (5–8)
Grandfather said the Indians must stick to the old ways. The
people at the white man's school had no knowledge of or respect
for any of the Indian traditions. Wabus' father, White Sky, said he
had to go to the school. The dream of the blue heron showed that
Wabus was to be the link between old and new in this story set in
Wisconsin in 1905.

BARRIE, JAMES M.   *Peter Pan*
Grosset (Tempo), 60¢   (4–6)
The list of characters almost tells the story: Peter Pan, a boy who
wouldn't grow up; Wendy, Michael, and John; Captain Hook,
Indians, and the fairy, Tinker Bell.

BAUDOUY, MICHEL-AIME   *More Than Courage*
Harcourt (Voyager), 60¢   (6 up)
Thirty-fourth in a Latin class of 34, Mick Martel is a born mechanic. Ignoring the class-conscious prejudices of his family, Mick
joins three neighborhood boys in resurrecting an old motorcycle
and racing it cross-country.

BAUM, L. FRANK   *The Marvelous Land of Oz*   Illus. by John R.
Neill.
Scholastic (Starline), 60¢   (3–5)
Tip, Jack Pumpkinhead, and the Saw Horse travel to Emerald City
to ask the Scarecrow's help just as an army of girls revolts and
drives the Scarecrow off his throne. With the Tin Woodman's help,
the girls themselves are overthrown, and Ozma, lost Princess of
Oz, returns as rightful ruler.

BAUM, L. FRANK   *The Wizard of Oz*   Illus. by W. W. Denslow.
Avon (Camelot), 60¢   (3–5)
Children who enjoy the annual television presentation of the
motion picture will be pleased by the book, which, while not quite
as climactic, contains more entrancing incidents.

BECKER, CHARLOTTE   *A Chimp in the Family*   Illus. by Seymour
Fleishman.
Scholastic, 50¢   (3–5)
Problems abound for the Davis family when father brings funlov-
ing Maggie, a chimp, home to their small apartment.

BEIM, LORRAINE   *Triumph Clear*
Harcourt (Voyager), 65¢   (5 up)
Marsh Evans, lame from polio, becomes a patient at the Georgia

Warm Springs Foundation. Her impatience to be cured completely and immediately so she can become an actress leads her into a variety of situations, pleasant and unpleasant, before she finally accepts her disability and adjusts to it.

Benary-Isbert, Margot *Blue Mystery* Illus. by E. Arno.
Harcourt (Voyager), 75¢ (5–7)
Germany before World War I is the scene of a family story with a touch of mystery. Annegret with the help of Cara, her great dane dog, is able to solve the mystery of the theft of her father's newly developed blue gloxinia. Translated from German by Clara and Richard Winston.

Benary-Isbert, Margot *The Long Way Home*
Scholastic, 75¢ (6 up)
Chris, an escapee from East Germany, finds that something different—such as the American way of doing things—can also be nice as he searches for a permanent home, first in Chicago and then in California.

Bennett, Anna Elizabeth *Little Witch*
Scholastic (Starline), 60¢ (4–6)
A young witch, who wants to see a fairy and be like a normal little girl, tries to undo the evil of her witch mother and gets her wishes granted.

Best, Herbert *Desmond and the Peppermint Ghost* Illus. by Lilian Obligado.
Viking (Seafarer), 65¢ (4–6)
Dog detectives find it hard to detect when their boys are in school, but Desmond tracks a peppermint smell and, aided by his boy, Gus, and the other dogs of the gang and their owners, solves the mystery of the disappearing peppermint patties.

Best, Herbert *Desmond the Dog Detective: The Case of the Lone Stranger* Illus. by Lilian Obligado.
Viking (Seafarer), 65¢ (4–6)
Desmond and Gus loved to play cops and robbers, but their lives suddenly changed when they encounter the real thing.

Blanton, Catherine *Hold Fast to Your Dreams*
WSP (Archway), 60¢ (6 up)
Emmy Lou decides that to become a ballerina she will leave her native Alabama and go to school in Arizona where there is no segregation. But life isn't that simple.

BOLTON, IVY *Wayfaring Lad*

WSP (Archway), 60¢ (4–6)

Richard Nolan has as enemies the citizens of the pioneer town who have exiled him for being a wastrel and laggard, the Chickamauga Indians, a half-breed Indian agent, and most of the French settlement. Befriended by the Cherokee Indians, he proves himself reliable and hardworking as he aids a fatherless French family.

BOND, GLADYS BAKER *A Head on Her Shoulders* Illus. by R. Kennedy

WSP (Archway), 60¢ (5–7)

When one's younger sister has more common sense than you and continually proves it, it takes a trip by boxcar from Nebraska to Oregon in charge of three children and the livestock to prove that one does have a head on her shoulders.

BOND, MICHAEL *A Bear Called Paddington* Illus. by Peggy Fortrum.

Dell (Yearling), 65¢ (3–5)

Paddington, a talking bear, arrives in London as a stowaway from Peru and is adopted by the Browns. As he tries to adapt to life in the Brown household, he runs into problems with escalators, supercilious store clerks, paint remover, and other human concerns.

BONHAM, FRANK *The Mystery of the Red Tide* Illus. by Brinton Turkle.

Scholastic, 60¢ (4–6)

A mysterious and exciting adventure begins for Tommy when he goes to live with his marine-biologist uncle in California.

BOSTON, L. M. *The River at Green Knowe* Illus. by P. Boston.

Harcourt (Voyager), 60¢ (5–7)

Three children—Ida, oriental Ping, and Polish Oskar—on a summer holiday find that exploration of the river at Green Knowe can provide many experiences in the land of fancy.

BRADBURY, BIANCA *Two on an Island*

Scholastic (Starline), 60¢ (4–5)

The adults fussed about two children stranded for four days on a sandbar island in sight of the city. But despite the hunger, thirst, sunburn, and fear, sullen, argumentative Jeff felt closer to his sister, Trudy, whom he normally disliked, than he did when they were safe at home.

BRINK, CAROL RYRIE *Baby Island* Illus. by Moneta Barnett.
Scholastic, 60¢ (4–6)
Twelve-year-old Mary and 10-year-old Jean rescue four babies
during a shipwreck and land on a tropical island where they live
happily for three months. During that time they convert a self-
exiled English seaman from a child hater to a baby lover.

BRINK, CAROL RYRIE *Caddie Woodlawn*
Macmillian (Collier), 95¢ (4–6)
Wisconsin in 1864 is a wonderful place to live for red-haired
Caddie, who runs wild with her two brothers until the visit of an
eastern cousin shows Caddie that there are things to be said in
favor of being ladylike. Awarded the Newbery Medal in 1936.

BRINK, CAROL RYRIE *The Highly Trained Dogs of Professor Petit*
Illus. by Robert Henneberger.
Scholastic, 60¢ (4–6)
Even very highly trained dogs are no competition for a show
featuring a tiger, and Professor Petit and his traveling show are
almost out of business until they meet Willie and the serious
townspeople of Puddling Center.

BROOKS, WALTER R. *Freddy the Detective*
Scholastic, 60¢ (4–6)
Inspired by Sherlock Holmes, Freddy, a pig, turns his barnyard
friends into detectives to solve problems such as a missing toy
train, a missing baby rabbit, and a bank robbed by two humans.

BRYANT, CHESTER *The Lost Kingdom* Illus. by M. Ayer.
WSP (Archway), 60¢ (6–9)
Rodmika knows more about the jungle than the oldest man in the
village. He traces an ancient roadway into the jungle, thus solving
the problems of his heritage and laying out a route for a modern
highway in this story of modern India.

BUCHAN, BRYAN *The Forgotten World of Uloc* Illus. by Kathryn
Cole.
Scholastic. 60¢ (4–6)
Two children meet a tiny, strange man whose plight sets them on a
daring and dangerous adventure. The story theme brings to light
pollution problems and man's attitude toward them.

BUCK, PEARL S. *The Big Wave* Illus. by Kazue Mizamura.
Scholastic (Starline), 60¢ (4–7)
"We love life because we live in danger." The precarious living of

the Japanese caught between volcano and sea is the theme of a beautiful story. After Jiya's family is killed by a tidal wave, he retreats from the sea physically and spiritually until its call is too strong for him to resist.

BUCK, PEARL S. *The Water-buffalo Children and the Dragon Fish* Illus. by Ester B. Bird and William A. Smith.
Dell (Yearling), 50¢ (3–5)
Each of these two stories deal with the same situation: the first encounter of Chinese children with a white child. In the first, the three children are equally curious about the properties of a magic stone. In the second, a Chinese and a white girl, tired of their brothers, run away planning to pawn a "stone fish" they've found.

BUFF, MARY, AND BUFF, CONRAD *The Apple and the Arrow*
Scholastic, 60¢ (4–6)
Walter Tell, son of William, tells of the freeing of the first three Swiss cantons from Austrian rule.

BULLA, CLYDE ROBERT *Down the Mississippi*
Scholastic, 60¢ (3–5)
The family's plan to turn Erik into a farmer by letting him see for himself how hard life on the river is backfires as Erik, inspired by the hard work and exciting incidents, decides he belongs to the roving side of the family like cousin Gunder.

BULLA, CLYDE ROBERT *Eagle Feather*
Scholastic (Starline), 60¢ (3–5)
A modern Navajo boy overcomes obstacles put in his way by cousin Crook Nose and gets to go to school.

BULLA, CLYDE ROBERT *Riding the Pony Express* Illus. by Grace Paull.
Scholastic (Starline), 60¢ (3–5)
Dick, at first resentful of the Nebraska prairies, of his father's frequent absences on the Pony Express run, and of the disruption of his home life is led to see the thrill and value of the Express when he has to make the run one day.

BULLA, CLYDE ROBERT *Star of Wild Horse Canyon* Illus. by Grace Paull.
Scholastic (Starline), 50¢ (3–5)
Danny helps capture some wild horses and gets one for his own.

BULLA, CLYDE ROBERT *The Sword in the Tree* Illus. by Paul Galdone.

Scholastic (Starline), 60¢ (3–5)
Shan regains his lost title and castle after the disappearance of his father with the help of Sir Gareth, knight of the Round Table.

BURNETT, FRANCES HODGSON *A Little Princess*

Grosset (Tempo), 50¢ (5–6)
A vivid imagination and the attitude of a princess help Sara Crewe through her ordeal as her fortunes change and she tumbles from the lofty position of wealthiest girl in a private school to the lowly one of half-starved kitchen drudge and then is sky-rocketed back up again.

BURNFORD, SHEILA *The Incredible Journey*

Bantam (Pathfinder), 75¢ (5 up)
An enthralling, realistic story of the 300-mile journey across the Canadian wastes made by a Siamese cat, an old English bull terrier, and a young Labrador retriever to return to their home.

BURTON, HESTER *Castors Away* Illus. by Victor G. Ambrus

Dell (Yearling), 75¢ (6 up)
The Battle of Trafalgar, life as a seaman, and life as an apprentice surgeon are all depicted in a story about a family of children who twice save the life of an British soldier.

BUTLER, BEVERLY *Light a Single Candle*

(Archway), 60¢ (5 up)
It seemed that fate had struck a cruel blow to Cathy, who at 14 lost her sight. But a ray of hope came to her life when she attended a school for the blind and met Trudy, her seeing-eye dog.

BUTTERWORTH, OLIVER *The Enormous Egg* Illus. by Louis Darling.

Scholastic, 75¢ (4–6)
After the problem of getting the egg to hatch is solved, there is the problem of what to do with what hatched out of it. The world's only living Triceratops causes problems for Nate Twitchell, for the New Hampshire community in which he lives, for the scientists of the world, and even for the Congress of the United States.

BYARS, BETSY *The Midnight Fox* Illus. by Ann Grifalconi.

Viking (Seafarer), 75¢ (4–6)
Tommy had always lived in the city, and it was with some misgivings that he went to spend the summer on his uncle's farm.

His adventures and thoughts on farm life are related in amusing fashion.

CALHOUN, MARY *The House of Thirty Cats* Illus. by Mary Chalmers.
(Archway), 60¢ (4–6)
Miss Tabitha and her 30 cats were a source of interest and joy to Sarah. But happiness is threatened when a mean neighbor tries to eliminate the pets. This story for cat lovers contains some good cat care information.

CALHOUN, MARY *Katie John*
Scholastic, 60¢ (4–6)
The adventures of impetuous and headstrong Katie John are a delight to read. Life in Missouri can be as interesting as life in California, and transplanted Katie John proves it.

CAMERON, ELEANOR *The Wonderful Flight to the Mushroom Planet*
Scholastic, 75¢ (4–6)
Tycho M. Bass, a native of the planet Basidium-X, enlists the aid of two boys to fly to the previously undiscovered earth satellite to save his people.

CAMPBELL, HOPE *Why Not Join the Giraffes?*
Dell (Yearling), 75¢ (5–9)
This humorous story tells of a little girl who wishes just once she could have an "average family." But, with an artistic mother, a father who writes, and a brother who belongs to a rock group, she doesn't stand much of a chance.

CANFIELD, DOROTHY *Understood Betsy* Illus. by Catherine Barnes.
Grosset (Tempo), 60¢ (5–8)
Nine-year-old Elizabeth Ann, who has never been allowed to do a thing or think a thought all by herself, goes to live with Vermont cousins who turn out to be the world's best child psychologists by pure instinct.

CARLSEN, RUTH CHRISTOFFER *Mr. Pudgins*
Scholastic, 60¢ (4–5)
The black smoke from Mr. Pudgin's pipe signaled marvelous adventures—such as a flight in a flying bathtub or a visit from the mirror children or a dodo bird—for the children for whom he was babysitting.

CARLSON, NATALIE SAVAGE *A Brother for the Orphelines* Illus. by Garth Williams.
Dell (Yearling), 75¢ (3–5)
A baby boy left at the gate of the girls' orphanage helps the orphanage move from a crumbling, mice-infested slum into a castle.

CARLSON, NATALIE SAVAGE *The Empty Schoolhouse* Illus. by John Kaufmann.
Dell (Yearling), 75¢ (4–6)
The desegregation of the Catholic school in French Grove, Louisiana, is not the peaceful process the community expects. Lullah Royall loses her best white friend and is the only student in school until the agitators are uncovered.

CARMER, CARL *A Flag for the Fort*
WSP (Archway), 50¢ (4–6)
Caroline, her mother, and grandmother make the huge flag that flies above Fort McHenry during the War of 1812 and inspires "The Star-Spangled Banner."

CARMER, CARL *Hurricane Luck* Illus. by Jerry Robinson.
Scholastic, 60¢ (3–5)
A hurricane off the Florida coast, though devastating in its physical destruction, changes the luck of the Tebo family for the better.

CARROLL, LEWIS *Alice in Wonderland: Through the Looking-Glass*
Airmont, 50¢; Macmillan (Collier), 65¢; NAL (Signet), 50¢; Penguin (Puffin), $1.25; St. Martin's 95¢ Lancer, 60¢ (4–7)
These fantasies are still among the greatest children's classics. In the first there's the mad tea party, the poem, "You are old, Father William," the Cheshire cat, and the rest of the deck of cards. The second of Alice's journeys involves her with chess set royalty, Jabberwocky, Tweedledum, and Tweedledee, Humpty Dumpty, "The Walrus and the Carpenter," and other poems.

CARROLL, LILLIAN *Greek Slave Boy* Illus. by Robert Geary.
Scholastic, 75¢ (6–8)
Pheidias, young son of a rich Greek family, is captured by pirates and sold into slavery in this exciting book about ancient Rome.

CAUDILL, REBECCA *The Best-Loved Doll*
Scholastic, 60¢ (2–4)
Betsy must choose one doll to go to a party at which prizes will be

given for the best dressed, the oldest, and so forth. The choice is difficult because her dolls are so special each one could win.

CHASTAIN, MADYE LEE *Emmy Keeps a Promise* Illus. by the author.
Harcourt (Voyager), 75¢ (4–6)
New York in 1850 is no place for two girls to live alone, and teaching is regarded only as a pastime until marriage. So 11-year-old Emmy promises her aunt that she'll get her beautiful sister married as soon as possible.

CHRISTOPHER, MATT *Break for the Basket*
Scholastic, 50¢ (4–6)
Emmett Torrance is almost too shy to play basketball. Mr. G. is a failure as a painter. Put the two together, and the problems of both are solved.

CHRISTOPHER, MATT *Touchdown for Tommy*
Scholastic, 50¢ (3–5)
Tommy knows that he plays football too rough and breaks rules, but, worried about leaving his foster home, he forgets to be careful.

CLAIR, ANDREE *Bemba: An African Adventure* Illus. by H. Johnson.
Harcourt (Voyager), 60¢ (4–6)
Bemba lives in the Congo just before it becomes independent. Fake witch doctors and French colonialists complicate things for an African tribe on the edge of civilization. Translated from the French by Marie Pensot.

CLARK, ANN NOLAN *Secret of the Andes* Illus. by Jean Charlot.
Viking (Seafarer), 75¢ (5–7)
Cusi, an Inca Indian boy, lives high in the mountains with an old Indian herder. They guard the precious llama flock. There Cusi learns the customs and lore of the Inca Indians. The young reader will be enchanted by the Inca songs and the vivid descriptions of the wild and beautiful grandeur of the Andes. Awarded the Newbery Medal in 1953.

CLARKE, ARTHUR C. *Dolphin Island: A Story of the People of the Sea*
Berkley, 75¢ (4–6)
Descriptions of sea life surrounding a coral island round out a mild

science fiction story based on the idea of men's communicating with dolphins through computerized translation of taped speech. Not as exciting as the truth.

Cleary, Beverly *Ellen Tebbits* Illus. by Louis Darling.

Scholastic, 60¢ (3–5)
Third grade brought Ellen Tebbits a new best friend and many problems concerning such things as winter underwear, matching dresses that don't match, and giant belts. Heartbreakingly funny.

Cleary, Beverly *Fifteen*

Scholastic, 60¢ (6 up)
The author realistically portrays the joys and heartaches of being 15 and having your first boyfriend.

Cleary, Beverly *Henry and the Clubhouse* Illus. by Louis Darling.

Scholastic, 60¢ (3–5)
Ramona, the new dog in the neighborhood, his paper route, and the new clubhouse he wants to build create too many problems for Henry Huggins to handle.

Cleary, Beverly *Henry and the Paper Route* Illus. by Louis Darling.

Scholastic, 60¢ (3–5)
Henry Huggins wanted a paper route. Among the things standing in his way were four kittens, a new neighbor boy, and Beezus' little sister.

Cleary, Beverly *Henry Huggins* Illus. by Louis Darling.

Scholastic, 50¢ (3–5)
Ribsy, guppies, night crawlers, and a pink dog humorously complicate Henry's life at age eight.

Cleary, Beverly *Ramona the Pest* Illus. by Louis Darling.

Scholastic, 60¢ (3–5)
Ramona has always been known as a pest, and when she starts kindergarten, things go from bad to worse.

Clymer, Eleanor *The Big Pile of Dirt* Illus. by Ben Shecter.

Scholastic, 50¢ (2–4)
In a child's mind a pile of dirt can be a rather pleasant and diversified play area. But should someone try to take the dirt away, there certainly will be a fight for it.

CLYMER, ELEANOR *My Brother Stevie*
Scholastic, 60¢ (4–6)
"Take care of your brother," Annie Jenner was told by her mother
before she deserted them. Nine-year-old Stevie, on the verge of
becoming delinquent, is more than 12-year-old Annie can handle,
and Grandma, who smacks Stevie, is no help. The situation
improves—but is not solved—with the help of an understanding
third-grade teacher.

CLYMER, ELEANOR *The Trolley Car Family*
Scholastic, 75¢ (4–6)
In a summer home made out of Pa's old trolley car, the Parker
family finds new friends and a country way of life, and they
change the life of a neighbor, Mr. Jefferson, completely.

COATSWORTH, ELIZABETH *Jock's Island* Illus. by Lilian Obligado.
Viking (Seafarer), 65¢ (4–6)
A twist of fate leaves Jock, a sheep dog, alone on an island. A new
life begins when he is found by a young boy and comes to
understand the meaning of love. Pencil illustrations add to the
warmth of the story.

COATSWORTH, ELIZABETH *Old Whirlwind*
Scholastic, 50¢ (3–6)
A fictionalized account of some experiences of Davy Crockett's
childhood including a trip with a drover, a shooting match, and an
escape through the snow to save the life of Old Whirlwind, his dog.

COLLODI, C. *The Adventures of Pinocchio*
Airmont, 60¢ (3–6)
Willful, lazy, and disobedient, Pinocchio has many unpleasant
adventures from which he learns nothing until it's almost too late.

COLMAN, HILA *Julie Builds Her Castle*
Dell (Laurel-Leaf), 50¢ (6 up)
Julie, age 16 and a conformist, almost hates her artist father at
times. When the family moves to Provincetown, Julie falls in love
with Pete, son of a Portuguese fisherman, who seems to hate his
nonconformist brother Joe. After Joe steals a boat, the relation-
ships of all those concerned begin to untangle.

CORBETT, SCOTT *The Lemonade Trick* Illus. by Paul Galdone.
Scholastic, 50¢ (3–5).
An old chemistry set given Kirby by a strange old lady causes

magical happenings to Kirby, his dog Waldo, and the Sunday school pageant.

Dawson, A. J. *Finn, the Wolfhound*
Harcourt (Voyager), 75¢ (6 up)
A wolfhound bred for dog shows in England but driven by circumstance to run wild in Australia is brutally treated in a small circus and breaks free to lead a wild dog pack. Most poignant is the detailing of the dog's relationship with man—individually and collectively.

Day, Veronique *Landslide!* Illus. by Margot Tomes.
Dell (Yearling), 75¢ (5–7)
A group of children are trapped in a hut covered by a landslide. Although they have food, they have no light. Characterization is handled very well.

Defoe, Daniel *Robinson Crusoe*
NAL (Signet), 60¢; Penguin (Puffin), 95¢ (6 up)
Twenty-five years on a tropical desert island give Robinson Crusoe plenty of time to accomplish his daily tasks of providing himself with food and shelter and to strengthen his religious faith.

DeLeeuw, Adele *Blue Ribbons for Meg*
Scholastic (Starline), 50¢ (4–6)
Nine-year-old Meg from Boston, who reads and knits, comes to live on a cavalry post in the Dakotas with "Indians and horses and things" that she fears. A puppy, a pony, and a stuffed teddy bear help her enjoy her life there.

Dickens, Charles *A Christmas Carol* Illus. by Charles Beck.
Airmont, 50¢; Pyramid, 35¢; WSP (Archway), 50¢
Scrooge's experiences with the ghosts of Christmas awaken forgotten memories and frighten him, thereby causing him to change his personality and outlook on life.

Dillon, Eilis *The Singing Cave*
Dell (Laurel-Leaf), 50¢ (5–7)
An Irish lad discovers an ancient Viking vessel in a cave on his island and, when it is stolen, follows it to France, thereby uncovering a villain in his village.

Dodge, Mary Mapes *Hans Brinker or the Silver Skates*
Airmont, 60¢ (5–7)
In addition to the famous race for the silver skates, there is a

double plot—a skating trip by a group of boys, which enables the author to discourse on the people and events of Dutch history and art, and an intriguing mystery involving Hans's injured father, some lost money, and a mysterious silver watch.

DU BOIS, WILLIAM PENE *The Twenty-one Balloons*
                                        Dell (Yearling), 95¢ (5 up)
Professor Sherman starts out to take a balloon trip across the Pacific and is picked up three weeks later in the Atlantic amid the debris of 21 balloons. In between, the reader finds dozens of uses for balloons and learns about volcanic erruption on Krakatoa. Awarded the Newbery Medal in 1948.

EAGER, EDWARD *Knight's Castle* Illus. by N. M. Bodecker.
                                        Harcourt (Voyager), 75¢ (5–7)
Three magical adventures based on Ivanhoe interfered with by four modern children.

EDELL, CELESTE *A Present from Rosita* Illus. by E. C. Fax.
                                        WSP (Archway), 60¢ (4–6)
A gently told story of the problems encountered by Puerto Ricans adjusting to New York City. Children seeing the problems through Rosita's eyes should be much more tolerant.

ELTING, MARY *All Aboard: The Trains that Built America*
                                        Scholastic, 95¢ (4–6)
This is the exciting story of the rise of the steam train, the origin of the trains we know today. Those were the dangerous days when men fought and died to build America's railroad system.

EMERSON, CAROLINE D. *The Magic Tunnel*
                                        Scholastic, 60¢ (3–5)
John and Sarah find themselves transported to New Amsterdam in 1664. Thrilled and puzzled by life in the Dutch community, they confuse their unknowing new parents by their peculiar ignorance of·everyday things, such as how to spin or why there are no forks on the table.

ENRIGHT, ELIZABETH *The Four-story Mistake* Illus. by the author.
                                        Dell (Yearling), 65¢ (4–6)
Musician Rush, actress Mona, artist and dancer Randy, seven-year-old Oliver, and their parents move into the Four-story Mistake, which allows them both to pursue their individual interest and to enjoy life together as a family.

ENRIGHT, ELIZABETH *Gone-away Lake* Illus. by Beth and Joe Krush.

Harcourt (Voyager), 75¢ (4–6)
No magic—just earthly fun—when Portia and Julian discover some brokendown summer houses on the edge of a bog and find that two of them are inhabited by a brother and sister who prefer life as it was at the turn of the century.

ENRIGHT, ELIZABETH *The Saturdays* Illus. by the author.

Dell (Yearling), 65¢ (4–6)
The Melendy children pool their allowances, and each does something special on a Saturday, in this first book of the series. As usual with the Melendys, simply visiting the art museum or opera turns into an unexpected adventure.

ENRIGHT, ELIZABETH *Then There Were Five*

Dell (Yearling), 75¢ (4–7)
Contributions to the war effort bring the Melendys into contact with their neighbors, especially Mark Herron, a mistreated orphan.

ESTES, ELEANOR *The Moffats* Illus. by Louis Slobodkin.

Harcourt (Voyager), $1.25 (4–6)
The four Moffats and their mother are not poverty-stricken, merely poor, and Jane, the next to youngest, thinks she can stand that. The shadow over their lives is that their beloved old yellow house is going to be sold and they'll have to move.

ESTES, ELEANOR *The Witch Family* Illus. by E. Ardizzone.

Harcourt (Voyager), 75¢ (3–5)
The pictures Amy draws banish Old Witch to a glass hill where she is eventually joined by Little Witch Girl and Baby Witch and guarded by Malachi, the spelling bee. An interweaving of fantasy and reality.

FARJEON, ELEANOR *The Glass Slipper* Illus. by E. Shepard.

Grosset (Tempo), 50¢ (3–6)
A delightful enlargement of the Cinderella story, leaving bones intact but padding the characters.

FAULKNER, GEORGENE, AND BECKER, JOHN *Melindy's Medal*

WSP (Archway), 60¢ (3–5)
Grandmother often told Melindy that her great-grandfather, her grandfather, and her father won medals for bravery in the field of

battles. What could Melindy do to win a medal? All she's really good at is music, and Melindy's music helps her win a medal for just pure bravery. Incidentally, Melindy and her family are black.

FEAGLES, ANITA *Casey, The Utterly Impossible Horse*

Scholastic, 60¢ (2–4)

A horse of your own isn't as much fun as you might imagine if the horse demands to be called Kitty Cat and to wear a pair of striped pajamas, sun glasses, and a party hat.

FEAGLES, ANITA *Twenty-Seven Cats Next Door* Illus. by Baron Storey.

Scholastic (Starline), 60¢ (3–4)

The right of an individual to own 27 cats versus the nuisance caused the community poses problems for Jim, whose next-door neighbor, Mrs. Ames, takes in any stray cat that comes along.

FIEDLER, JEAN *The Green Thumb Story* Illus. by Wayne Blickenstaff.

Scholastic (Starline), 50¢ (2–3)

When Peter's mother tells him people need a green thumb to grow flowers, he sets out on a search for someone with this most unusual type of thumb.

FISHER, AILEEN *Skip*

Scholastic, 60¢ (4–6)

A blind dog has no place on a farm where everything has to pay its way. When Krissy realizes her dog Skip is blind and won't be able to keep the cows, she tries to keep his blindness a secret.

FISHER, CYRUS *The Avion My Uncle Flew*

Scholastic, 75¢ (5–7)

John has a busy summer in store for him. He must walk for two miles on his damaged leg, learn enough French to write his mother a two-page letter, keep an eye on his uncle who is building a new type of glider, and solve the mystery of Mr. Fischfasse. John accomplishes all his aims, and the reader learns enough French to read John's essay at the end of the book.

FITZHUGH, LOUISE *Harriet the Spy*

Dell (Yearling), 95¢ (4–6)

You can never begin too young to train to be a spy. The trouble comes when Harriet's classmates read her overly frank comments about them in her private notebook.

Fleming, Ian *Chitty Chitty Bang Bang*

NAL (Signet), 75¢ (5 up)

A car with secret knobs, buttons, and levers drives and flies the Potts family into unorthodox situations, including one with international thieves.

Fon Eisen, Anthony *Bond of the Fire* Illus. by W. T. Mars.

Dell (Yearling), 75¢ (5–7)

Ash, a Cro-Magnon Boy, is adopted by a dog that has already been tamed by another tribe. The dog's aid in hunting makes life for Ash's tribe much easier. A well-written story assuming Cro-Magnon could reason like modern men and including the excitment of a flood and the unfolding of the first ideas of a spiritual life.

Forbes, Esther *Johnny Tremain* Illus. by Lynd Ward.

Dell (Yearling), 95¢ (6 up)

The Boston Tea Party and the battles of Lexington and Concord are the big events in this colorful picture of life in pre-revolutionary Boston. Johnny's future as a silversmith is destroyed when his hand is burned by molten silver. In making a new life for himself, he is enveloped by the political events of his time. Awarded the Newbery Award in 1944.

Fox, Paula *The Stone-faced Boy* Illus. by Donald A. Mackag.

Scholastic, 50¢ (4–6)

Gus, the third of five children, feels insecure and unsure of himself. Holding his feelings inside, he is unable to even smile until an exciting search for a pet he loves releases his emotions.

Friedman, Frieda *Dot for Short* Illus. by Carolyn Haywood.

Scholastic, 60¢ (4–6)

It's little, dark, plain, shy Dot who bears the burden of the knowledge of her father's illness and tries to earn money to help. The setting is Third Avenue in New York.

Friedman, Frieda *Janitor's Girl* Illus. by Mary Stevens.

Scholastic, 60¢ (4–6)

Snubbed because she is the janitor's girl, Sue in turn snubs the immigrant daughter of her father's assistant until everyone discovers that it's what you are as a person that counts.

Friedman, Frieda *A Sundae With Judy*

Scholastic, 60¢ (4–6)

Judy and her new Chinese friend, forced out of the Saturday Club by prejudice, scarcely miss the others as they work to help a father and his children when the mother is in the hopsital.

FRITZ, JEAN *Brady*

Scholastic, 75¢ (4–7)

Brady can't keep quiet. His chatter forces the closing of one Underground Railroad station, so it is no surprise that his preacher father tries to keep all other information about runaway slaves away from him.

GARRETT, HELEN *Angelo, The Naughty One* Illus. by Leo Politi.

Viking (Seafarer), 95¢ (K–2)

Angelo's fear of water prompts him to run away from home. But complications arise when he is "captured" by a band of soldiers who decide he is so dirty that they will give him a bath.

GATES, DORIS *Blue Willow* Illus. by P. Lantz.

Viking (Seafarer), 75¢ (3–6)

Janey Larkin, whose father is a migrant worker, yearns for the day when her family will live in a house and be able to stay as long as they want. A touching story of the lack of security felt by migrant children.

GATES, DORIS *Little Vic* Illus. by K. Seredy.

WSP (Archway), 60¢ (5–7)

Pony, a small Negro groom, follows Little Vic, grandson of Man o' War, from owner to owner, believing in him even though he continually loses unimportant races. Finally, Pony himself rides Little Vic in the biggest race and wins.

GATES, DORIS *Sensible Kate* Illus. by M. Torroy.

Viking (Seafarer), 75¢ (4–6)

Kate is sensible but she wants to be pretty and cute. Her sensibleness, however, earns her adopted parents and grandparents, a boyfriend, and success for her new father.

GEORGE, JEAN *My Side of the Mountain*

Scholastic, 75¢ (5–7)

A city boy survives the winter in the wilds of the Catskill Mountains, living in a hollowed-out tree, hunting, trapping, and eating only the food of the wild.

GIPSON, FRED *Old Yeller*

Harper, 60¢ (5–7)

A big, ugly, yellow dog with no tail and a chewed-off ear, the biggest thief in the area, attaches himself to the Coates family in Texas after the Civil War. Time and again he helps the boys, Travis and Little Arliss, in their encounters with not-so-tame domestic animals—wild bulls and wild hogs and with bears and wolves.

Gipson, Fred *Savage Sam*
Pocket, 60¢ (6 up)
Travis, Arliss, and Lisbeth are captured by Indians. Their only hope of being rescued is that Savage Sam, son of Old Yeller, may bring help.

Godden, Rumer *The Doll's House* Illus. by Tasha Tudor.
Viking (Seafarer), 95¢ (3–5)
This sensitive, memorable book brings to life a family of dolls and involves them in the human adventures of their young owners. The warm wisdom of this story will delight doll lovers everywhere.

Godden, Rumer *Mouse House* Illus. by Adrienne Adams.
Viking (Seafarer), 75¢ (2–4)
A happy solution to the problem of raising a large family of mice in one flowerpot is unintentionally found by Bonnie, the smallest mouse, who was always pushed out of the flowerpot.

Gottlieb, Robin *Mystery of the Silent Friends*
Scholastic (Starline), 60¢ (4–6)
Nina and Muffin decide there's a mystery present when two different men give the same name and the same reason for wanting to buy the beautiful Swiss automatons in Nina's father's antique shop.

Grahame, Kenneth *The Wind in the Willows*
Airmont, 75¢; Avon (Camelot), 60¢; Dell, 95¢; Grosset (Tempo), 60¢; Lancer, 60¢; NAL (Signet), 75¢; Scribner, $1.76 (5 up)
Using anthropomorphism is not the modern way to write animal stories, but let's let the children keep this classic in which Toad lives in a mansion and drives a car; Rat, Mole, and Badger have adventures along the river bank; and everyone talks and wears clothes.

Greene, Constance C. *A Girl Called Al* Illus. by Byron Barton.
Viking (Seafarer), 95¢ (5–8)
Al, daughter of a broken marriage, is intelligent, witty, and offbeat. Her friendship with a neighbor girl and the assistant

superintendent of her apartment house brings out her wisdom and provides some very interesting experiences.

GRIFFITHS, HELEN *The Greyhound*

Scholastic, 60¢ (4–6)

A London boy's love for a greyhound owned by someone else leads him into financial problems, involvement in a gang of petty thieves and bullies, and deceiving his parents.

HALE, LUCRETIA P. *Peterkin Papers*

Dover, $1.50 (5–7)

Any problem any member of the Peterkin family has is compounded by the contributions of the rest of the family and often has to be solved by the lady from Philadelphia. A foolishly funny collection of stories.

HALLQUIST, BRITT G. *Bettina's Secret* Illus. by Marjorie-Ann Watts.

Scholastic, 60¢ (4–6)

Little Bettina found the hospital to be a very lonely place until mysterious Nurse Julia visits her bedside late at night. Translated from Swedish by Anne Parker.

HAMILTON, VIRGINIA *The House of Dies Drear*

Macmillan (Collier), 95¢ (6–8)

Thomas's family moves into a haunted house complete with ghosts and hidden passageways. But the secret of this house, which served as a station on the Underground Railroad, involves a mysterious old caretaker and comes to a dramatic, almost theatrical climax.

HAMILTON, VIRGINIA *Zeely* Illus. by Symeon Shimin.

Scholastic, 60¢ (6 up)

While spending the summer on her uncle's farm, an imaginative black girl becomes convinced that the tall, graceful young woman who helps tend hogs nearby is in reality a Watusi queen. Both Geeder and Miss Zeely recognize the importance of being one's own self.

HAMORI, LÁSZLÓ *The Dangerous Journey* Illus. by W. J. Maro.

Harcourt (Voyager), 60¢ (6 up)

Latsi and Pishta are safely hidden in a boxcar leaving Hungary. Separated from Pishta, Latsi arrives in Vienna, where he falls into the hands of a blackmailer. Translated from the Swedish by Annabelle MacMillan.

HARKINS, PHILIP *Argentine Road Race*

Berkley, 50¢ (6 up)
Pedro Thompson acts as co-driver and mechanic for Senor Rosendo Fraga in the Argentine Grand Prix. Conflict between their personalities rides with them all the way and proves to be as trying as the nine-day race. It's colorful and exciting, with an unforgettable climax.

HAUGAARD, ERIC. C. *Orphans of the Wind* Illus. by Milton Johnson.

Dell (Yearling), 75¢ (5–7)
Twelve-year-old Jim sails on a British ship illegally carrying ammunition and powder to the Confederacy during the Civil War. Arguments on both sides of the Civil War question are presented by various crew members.

HENRY, MARGUERITE *Black Gold* Illus. by Wesley Dennis.

Rand, $1.50 (4–6)
Al Hoots wants to raise a winning race horse, Jaydee wants to ride one. How their dreams merge is revealed in this inspiring story of a spunky little race horse.

HENRY, MARGUERITE *Brighty of the Grand Canyon* Illus. by Wesley Dennis.

Rand, $1.50 (4–6)
A burro who was half-wild, half-free really roamed the Grand Canyon at the turn of the century. Brighty occasionally works for and with humans and aids in uncovering the murderer of his first friend.

HENRY, MARGUERITE *Justin Morgan Had a Horse* Illus. by Wesley Dennis.

Scholastic, 75¢ (4–6)
This inspiring story tells of an extraordinary little horse whose strength, stamina, and willingness to serve made him the sire of the famous breed of Morgan horses.

HENRY, MARGUERITE *King of the Wind* Illus. by Wesley Dennis

Rand, $1.50; Scholastic, 75¢ (5–8)
The Godolphin Arabian, who never raced but whose blood runs in the veins of most racers today, came from royal stables but became a mistreated cart horse before his lineage was recognized. Awarded the Newbery Medal in 1949.

HENRY, MARGUERITE *Misty of Chincoteague* Illus. by Wesley Dennis.

Rand, $1.50; Scholastic, 75¢ (5–8)
Paul and Maureen decide that during the annual Pony Penning

they will capture the Phantom who has twice eluded the men of Chincoteague. When Paul succeeds, he finds Phantom has a colt whom he names Misty. The story is based on fact and is beautifully illustrated.

HENRY, MARGUERITE   *Sea Star: Orphan of Chincoteague*   Illus.by Wesley Dennis.

Rand, $1.50; Scholastic, 75¢   (5–8)
Paul and Maureen sell Misty to a movie company. The empty space in their hearts is filled by an orphaned colt they find.

HENRY, MARGUERITE   *Stormy, Misty's Foal*   Illus. by Wesley Dennis.

Rand, $1.50; Scholastic, 75¢   (5–8)
Chincoteague is flooded, and the Beebe family's tension is further increased by the knowledge that Misty is due to foal at anytime.

HOFF, CAROL   *Johnny Texas*   Illus. by Bob Meyers.

Dell (Yearling), 75¢   (4–7)
A German family emigrates to Texas after the Alamo. Despite a saccharine ending, this story about emigrants who came here for freedom has a slightly different slant—youngsters who adapt easily and parents who aren't always so happy.

HOGARTH, GRACE   *The Funny Guy*

Scholastic, 75¢   (4–6)
Few readers will have as many reasons to be unhappy as Helen, whose mother has been in the hospital for three years and who is an outcast among her classmates and the brunt of their teasing and pranks. Although she eventually finds a friend, there are more troubles in store before her problems are cleared up.

HOOPES, NED, ED.   *The Wonderful World of Horses*

Dell (Laurel-Leaf), 50¢   (4–6)
Here are 15 superb horse stories by some of our most distinguished writers.

HUNT, IRENE   *Across Five Aprils*

Grosset (Tempo), 60¢   (5–8)
The Civil War is depicted from the viewpoint of Jethro Creighton, who has a brother on each side and a cousin who deserts and stays home on a southern Illinois farm as the man of the family after his father's stroke.

INYART, GENE   *Jenny*   Illus. by Nancy Grossman.

WSP (Archway), 60¢   (3–5)
Jenny's world seemed to be falling apart. Her special king-

dom—the overgrown backyard next door—was doomed by new neighbors who cleared it and a new brother who came home from the hospital and claimed all her parents' attention. But fortunately she met with some good fortune and discovered that life has many moments of joy and gladness.

IRVING, WASHINGTON   *The Legend of Sleepy Hollow & Other Stories*
Airmont, 50¢   (6 up)
A story for reading aloud just to hear the marvelous words. Although the Headless Horseman makes this a Halloween favorite, there is no reason to limit its appreciation to the month of October.

ISH-KISHOR, JUDITH   *Joel Is the Youngest*
WSP (Archway), 60¢   (4–6)
Joel, youngest son in a Spanish-Jewish family, wants very much to catch up with his older brothers and have his opinion valued by them. The stories his grandfather tells him of the contributions of Jews to early American history are the unexpected means to this end.

JACKSON, C. P., AND JACKSON, O. B.   *Hillbilly Pitcher*
Scholastic, 60¢   (4–6)
A few southern mannerisms in his speech make Wilson Hadley the butt of crude jokes about "cornpone" and "hillbilly" in his new school in the north. The same kind of teasing ruins his excellent control as a pitcher for the school baseball team. Wilson learns to turn this weakness to advantage both in school and on the field.

JACKSON, JESSE   *Call Me Charley*   Illus. by Doris Spiegel.
Dell (Yearling), 75¢   (6 up)
A realistic story of real boys, not stereotypes. Charley is the first Negro to go to school at Arlington Heights (Ohio) Junior High; George is the son of bigoted parents; and Tom is the son of an unprejudiced family. As Charley tries to fit into the community, Tom is sometimes on his side and sometimes on George's. At other times the three get along fine.

JACKSON, JESSE   *Tessie*   Illus. by Harold James.
Dell (Yearling), 75¢   (6–9)
Bright, talented Tessie wins a scholarship to an exclusive private school and must learn to reconcile the environment there with her home and family in Harlem.

JACKSON, WALTER *The Flight of the Doves*
Macmillan (Collier), 95¢ (5–8)
Orphaned Finn, twelve, and Derval, seven, escape the clutches of
their cruel uncle and courageously set out to find their grandmother who lives across the sea.

JAMES, WILL *Smoky, the Cowhorse*
Scribner, $2.45 (6 up)
Beginning as a detailed, knowledgeable description of training a
semi-wild horse to be a cow pony, the story then follows the usual
pattern of brutalization, mistreatment, and, eventually, recovery
of the animal by its original owner. Awarded the Newbery Medal
in 1927.

JANE, MARY C. *The Ghost Rock Mystery*
Scholastic (Starline), 60¢ (4–6)
Aunt Annabelle's venture trying to run a tourist home in northern
Maine will fail if the children can't find the cause of the continuing
rumors that the property is haunted.

JANE, MARY C. *Mystery at Shadow Pond*
Scholastic, 60¢ (4–6)
Margie, Neale, and Rupert solve the mystery of the missing letters.
The letters were from a now-famous artist, and possible thieves
include the miser next door and the dead artist's cousin.

JANE, MARY C. *Mystery by Moonlight*
Scholastic, 60¢ (4–6)
A very selective and very successful thief may cause Sheriff
Prescott to lose the election unless his son Conan and Conan's
friend Gail are right about their suspicions of the odd sounds
coming from a burned-out old mansion.

JOHNSON, ANNABEL, AND JOHNSON, EDGAR *The Grizzly* Illus. by
Gilbert Riswold.
Scholastic, 60¢ (5–7)
David, overprotected by his mother, is terrified of his father, whom
he hasn't seen for several years. A camping and fishing trip starts
as a nightmare until David discovers his courage and tests his
strength after his father is injured by a grizzly.

KASSIRER, NORMA *Magic Elizabeth* Illus. by Joe Krush.
Scholastic, 75¢ (4–6)
Long years ago a doll belonging to a girl named Sally disappeared

like magic from the top of the Christmas tree. A new Sally, who is staying with her old aunt in the same house, is determined to find the doll.

KÄSTNER, ERICH *Emil and the Detectives*

Scholastic, 60¢ (4–6)

Emil's money is stolen while he is on his way to visit Berlin. He sets out to recover it and meets a gang of boys, all of whom join the eventually successful search.

KENDALL, CAROL *The Gammage Cup* Illus. by E. Blegvad.

Harcourt (Voyager), 65¢ (5–7)

The Minnipins are little people who have lived so long in peace and safety that their rule of life is conformity and their concept of history is a wee bit confused. Four exiled nonconformists save the village when danger threatens. A delightful world of fantasy filled with engaging characters and amusing, original customs and manners.

KINNEY, HARRISON *The Lonesome Bear* Illus. by Harold Price.

Scholastic (Starline), 60¢ (3–5)

An outrageously social circus bear invades a household and eventually captures the hearts of everyone involved.

KIPLING, RUDYARD *Captains Courageous*

Airmont, 50¢ (6 up)

Heavy with dialect and details of commercial fishing, this is the story of how Harvey Cheyne, the pampered son of an American millionaire who thought money could buy everything, changed his sense of values during his enforced stay on a fishing boat.

KIPLING, RUDYARD *Jungle Books*

Airmont, 50¢; Dell (Laurel-Leaf), 50¢; Grosset (Tempo). 50¢; Lancer, 75¢; NAL (Signet), 50¢ (5–7)

Stories of Mowgli, the man-cub raised by wolves, his adventures with life in a village, and his return to the jungle; of the White Seal; of Rikki-Tikki-Tavis success in ridding his human's house and yard of Nag, the cobra and his family; and of Toomaii seeing the elephant dance.

KIPLING, RUDYARD *Just So Stories*

Airmont, 60¢; Camelot, 60¢; Schocken, $1.75 (3–5)

Marvelous explanations of how the camel got his hump or how the cat remains independent of man are beautiful for reading aloud and are just as good if read carefully to oneself.

KIPLING, RUDYARD *Kim*
Airmont, 50¢; Dell, 50¢; Macmillan (Collier), 65¢ (5 up)
The beautiful panorama of India in 1900, which is this book's strong point, is also its weakness, as it slows at times to a complete stop to unfold the plot of the wild, orphaned English boy who, disguised as a Tibetan lama's disciple, spies for the English.

KIRN, ANN *Two Pesos for Catalina* Illus. by the author.
Scholastic (Starline), 60¢ (2–4)
Catalina has two whole pesos to spend all for herself. She looks at everything for sale in the Mexican village before she finds just what she wants—red shoes.

KJELGAARD, JIM *Big Red*
Scholastic (Starline), 60¢ (6 up)
Danny, who with his father lives by hunting and trapping, is given charge of a neighbor's prize Irish setter who is being trained as a show dog. Although Danny's father prefers hounds, it is Big Red who helps Danny put an end to the old bear who has terrorized their area.

KJELGAARD, MIN *Irish Red*
Scholastic (Starline), 50¢ (6 up)
Danny and his father tangle with Mr. Haggins' nephew and dog trainer over the merits of English versus Irish setters and go back to the woods. Big Red's maverick son Mike follows them, and Danny finally comes to see Mike's natural abilities as a hunter.

KJELGAARD, JIM *Outlaw Red*
Scholastic, 50¢ (6 up)
Sean, another of Big Red's sons, is a perfect show dog. Accidentally abandoned in the wilderness, the kennel-raised animal learns how to live in the wild, seduces his show-dog mate out of her kennel, and outwits several men until found and recognized by his former kennel boy, also living the life of an outlaw.

KNIGHT, ERIC *Lassie Come Home*
Grosset (Tempo), 60¢ (4–6)
A collie, taken far from her young master to the north of Scotland, travels the length of Britain to return to what she considers home.

LAMB, CHARLES, AND LAMB, MARY *Tales From Shakespeare,* abridged ed.
Bantam (Pathfinder), 75¢
The familiar tales told by the Lambs are here supplemented by Elizabeth Donn's narratives of the rest of Shakespeare's plays.

LAMPMAN, EVELYN *The Shy Stegosaurus of Cricket Creek*
Scholastic, 75¢ (4–6)
No one believes Joan and Joey when they say they have found a
live, talking stegosaurus, so they decide to keep George a secret.
Joey wants to use George to make enough money so they and their
mother can stay on the ranch. All his plans fail, but George's plan
is more successful than is convenient.

LAUBER, PATRICIA *Clarence Goes to Town*
Scholastic, 60¢ (4–6)
Clarence and his family spend a month in New York where he
distinguishes himself by discovering the most desirable mousetrap
bait, by being the silent partner on the winning team in a quiz and
stunt contest, and by helping to uncover a ring of dog thieves.

LAUBER, PATRICIA *Clarence, the TV Dog*
Scholastic, 60¢ (4–6)
Funny short stories told by Patricia Logan about her dog Clarence.
Clarence, who likes to watch television (which the Logan family
doesn't have), catches a burglar by being too friendly and helps
reform various Logan aunts and uncles whose behavior has
complicated life for the Logan children.

LAWRENCE, MILDRED *Peachtree Island* Illus. by M. Stevens.
Harcourt (Voyager), 65¢ (3–5)
A pleasant story about a well-adjusted orphan who goes to live
with a cheerful uncle, the owner of a large peach orchard.
Believing Uncle Eben prefers a boy, Cissie works hard in the
orchard to prove she's as useful as a boy. Her only real problems
are caused by rabbits and by the teasing boy next door.

LAWSON, ROBERT *Rabbit Hill* Illus. by the author.
Dell (Yearling), 75¢ (4–6)
All the animals are excited about new folks coming to live in the
house on the hill. Although Little Georgie, the youngest son of
Mother and Father Rabbit, is the main character, there are also
skunks, wolves, a woodchuck, fox, and other animals who look
forward to harvesting the garden. Awarded the Newbery Medal in
1945.

LENSKI, LOIS *Blue Ridge Billy* Illus. by the author.
Dell (Yearling), 75¢ (4–6)
This regional novel focuses on Ashe County, North Carolina. From
his mother's side of the family, Billy has inherited a love of music,
but his father has forbidden him to play his simple homemade

instrument or to sing. To add to Billy's troubles, there is an illegal still in the hills. Although he doesn't know who is operating it, it may be his father.

LENSKI, LOIS *Cotton in My Sack*

Dell (Yearling), 65¢ (4–6)
Although all Miss Lenski's books end happily, there is more character development in this one than in most. Poor, white Arkansas sharecroppers profit from the help of the school teacher and Uncle Shine and work to become tenant farmers. A sympathetic but not blind portrayal of the lives of sharecroppers.

LENSKI, LOIS *Judy's Journey*

Dell (Yearling), 65¢ (4–6)
Judy's family spends a year as migrant workers going from Georgia to Florida and up the seacoast. Judy learns to accept transient contacts with people and not to dwell on the insecurity of life.

LENSKI, LOIS *Prairie School*

Dell (Yearling), 75¢ (4–6)
A prairie school in South Dakota during one of the worst winters in history is the focal point of the story. The weather is the villain, repeatedly attacking the area and stranding the children in school.

LENSKI, LOIS *Strawberry Girl*

Dell (Yearling), 75¢ (4–6)
There is a lot of action when the shiftless Slaters resent the coming of the Boyers to their Florida home. The Boyers plant crops, feed their animals, and fence the area; the Slaters poison the Boyer's mule, run their hogs and cattle through the planted fields, and try to burn the Boyers out. Awarded the Newbery Medal in 1946.

LEWIS, C. S. *The Horse and His Boy* Adapted from illus. by Pauline Baynes.

Macmillan (Collier), 95¢ (4 up)
The fifth in the series of *The Chronicles of Narnia*. Held captive in a strange country, Bree, a talking horse, and Shasta, the young boy, embark on a journey of escape. Excitement mounts as they encounter one danger after another.

LEWIS, C. S. *The Lion, the Witch and the Wardrobe* Adapted from illus. by Pauline Baynes.

Macmillan (Collier), 95¢ (6 up)
The first story for children by the famed English author and the

first in "The Chronicles of Narnia" series. The story takes place in a magical land where animals talk and creatures of all sorts live in harmony with one another except for a wicked witch who has cursed the land with eternal winter. Good triumphs, however, with the help of four brave children and the golden lion king.

LEWIS, C. S. *The Magician's Nephew* Adapted from illus. by Pauline Baynes.

Macmillan (Collier), 95¢ (4 up)
The sixth in "The Chronicles of Narnia" series. Two children begin a fantastic journey that unfolds into the story of Narnia's creation, a magical country where animals can talk.

LEWIS, C. S. *Prince Caspian* Adapted from illus. by Pauline Baynes.

Macmillan (Collier), 95¢ (6 up)
The second in "The Chronicles of Narnia" series. Once again good triumphs over evil when the rightful king is restored to his throne with the help of all the magical people on the island.

LEWITON, MINA *The Divided Heart*

Berkley, 50¢ (5–8)
Julie finds it terribly hard to accept the fact that her parents are separating. But a loving mother and a good friend help her learn to cope with what had to be.

LINDGREN, ASTRID *Pippi in the South Seas* Illus. by Louis S. Glanyman.

Viking (Seafarer), 75¢ (4–6)
Pippi, Tommy, and Anika visit the South Seas island on which Pippi's father is king of the cannibals. Pippi cries after she deprives a shark of Tommy for his breakfast, foils some pearl thieves, and has her own Christmas celebration in January. Translated from the Swedish.

LINDGREN, ASTRID *Pippi Longstocking* Illus. by Louis S. Glanyman.

Viking (Seafarer), 75¢ (4–6)
At the age of nine, Pippi has not a frustration in the world. She is the world's strongest girl, lives alone with absolutely no adult to tell her what to do, and has an utter disregard for cleanliness and truth. Naturally, she is a most wonderful neighbor for Tommy and Anika to have. Translated from the Swedish.

LINDGREN, ASTRID *Rasmus and the Vagabond* Illus. by E. Palm-quist.

WSP (Archway), 50¢ (4–6)

Rasmus, convinced he'll never be adopted, runs away from a Swedish orphanage to find a family for himself. Joining forces with Oscar, a singing tramp, he finds that they are prime suspects for several robberies in the neighborhood. Translated from the Swedish.

LOFTING, HUGH *Doctor Dolittle Tales*

Scholastic, 75¢ (4–6)

These tales are selections from *Doctor Dolittle: A Treasury.* Doctor Dolittle searches for a pushmi-pullyu in Africa and has many adventures on Spidermonkey Island.

LOFTING, HUGH *Doctor Dolittle's Circus*

Dell (Laurel-Leaf), 60¢ (4–6)

To raise money, Dr. Dolittle joins a circus to display the pushmi-pullyu. With difficulty he helps a seal escape across 40 miles of land so she can return to her husband in the Arctic. Finally he is forced to take over the badly run circus and applies his own unique ideas.

LOFTING, HUGH *Doctor Dolittle's Post Office*

Dell (Laurel-Leaf), 60¢ (4–6)

The doctor, on his way home from a visit to Africa, helps capture a slave ship and sets up a post office in the small African country of Fantippo. Developing a foreign mails department using birds as carriers, he also sets up a weather bureau based on the birds' reports; publishes an animals' magazine, including stories told by all his close friends; and saves a neighboring kingdom's economy by discovering how to fish for pearl oysters.

LOFTING, HUGH *Doctor Dolittle's Zoo*

Dell (Laurel-Leaf), 60¢ (4–7)

The doctor and Tommy stay home in this book, set up a home for native animals in the backyard, listen to various mouse tales, and solve the mystery of the peculiar behavior of the master of Moorsden Manor.

LOFTING, HUGH *The Story of Doctor Dolittle*

Dell (Yearling), 60¢ (4–7)

First book of the series, in which the doctor learns to talk to the animals, becomes a veterinarian, journeys to Africa to cure the sick monkeys, meets Prince Bumpo, and acquires the pushmi-pullyu.

Lofting, Hugh *The Voyages of Doctor Dolittle*
Dell (Laurel-Leaf), 60¢ (4–7)
Tommy Stubbins tells how he became the doctor's assistant; how they cleared Luke the Hermit of a murder charge; found Long Arrow, the world's greatest botanist who had disappeared; conversed with the doctor in Eagle Talk; stopped bullfighting in the Casa Blanca Island; and saved the natives of a floating island. Awarded the Newbery Medal in 1923.

Lomask, Milton *The Secret of Grandfather's Diary* Illus. by W. T. Maro.
WSP (Archway), 60¢ (4–6)
The mystery of who stole the toys from grandmother's house and why is solved in two days. In that short time Denny suspects Peter, Peter steals a kitten, Denny and Peter have a fight, Peter's mother is frightened by a phone call, and grandmother and Denny straighten everything out.

London, Jack *The Call of the Wild* and *White Fang*
Bantam (Pathfinder), 60¢ (6–9)
In the first of these two famous dog stories, Buck, a cross between a St. Bernard and a Scottish shepherd dog, is taken from the comforts of his California home to become an Alaskan sled dog. The brutal life forces him to leave humans and run with the wolves. In the second, White Fang, half-dog and half-wolf, despite brutal treatment, becomes domesticated through his love for a human.

Lord, Beman *Quarterback's Aim*
Scholastic, 50¢ (3–5)
Although he weighs only fifty-four pounds, Alan's experience as a paperboy has given him a good arm and he comes off the bench and wins the football game with one fine pass.

Lyons, Dorothy *Dark Sunshine* Illus. by Wesley Dennis.
Harcourt (Voyager), 75¢ (6 up)
Although severely crippled by polio, Blythe finds that life is worthwhile after she is given a horse. She not only trains the horse and rides it in the endurance race but works hard at many projects in school to win a scholarship for voice lessons.

McCLOSKEY, ROBERT *Homer Price* Illus. by the author.

Scholastic, 75¢ (4–6)

A collection of humorous stories concerning Homer Price, whose various uncles needed his help when the doughnut machine wouldn't stop, when the sheriff almost wins the ball of string contest, and when the people in Enders' Heights can't tell whose house is whose.

McCLOSKEY, ROBERT *More Homer Price* Illus. by the author.

Scholastic, 75¢ (4–6)

Grandpa Herc tells tall tales and Homer's other relatives involve him in even more unusual predicaments than before. Adapted from *Centerburg Tales.*

MacDONALD, GEORGE *At the Back of the North Wind* Illus. by the author.

Airmont, 60¢ (4–6)

Diamond has dreamlike adventures with the North Wind, who usually appears to him as a beautiful woman. He also has a very practical existence as the son of a driver of a horsedrawn cab in London.

MacDONALD, GEORGE *The Princess and the Curdie* Illus. by A. Hughes.

Penguin (Puffin), 95¢ (4–6)

A sequel to *The Princess and the Goblin.* Curdie, a miner and son of a miner, is again called to help the royal family. This time the princess is the mysterious grandmother of Curdie's princess, who has magical powers and appears in many forms to help Curdie as he travels to the royal city, accumulating 49 hideously ugly animals on the way. Eventually he saves the king's life and kingdom.

McGOVERN, ANN, ED. *Treasury of Christmas Stories* Illus. by David Lockhart.

Scholastic, 60¢ (4–6)

A collection of stories, poems, and Christmas carols—all well-known pieces.

MacGREGOR, ELLEN *Miss Pickerell and the Geiger Counter* Illus. by Paul Galdone.

Scholastic, 60¢ (4–6)

Elementary information about radiation, uranium, and atomic energy is worked into Pickerell's second adventure, which starts off innocently when she takes a cow to the veterinarian and ends with her becoming a deputy sheriff and discovering uranium.

MacGregor, Ellen *Miss Pickerell Goes to Mars* Illus. by Paul Galdone.

Scholastic, 60¢ (4–6)
Even though the reader is asked to believe that Miss P could unintentionally stow away on a rocket leaving for Mars from her own cow pasture with no contact with Mission Control, the story is enjoyable—and Miss P does get her now famous red rock collection.

MacGregor, Ellen *Miss Pickerell Goes to the Arctic* Illus. by Paul Galdone.

Scholastic, 60¢ (4–6)
Miss P goes along to the Arctic with a rescue crew, which then crashes and has to be rescued too.

MacGregor, Ellen *Miss Pickerell Goes Undersea* Illus. by Paul Galdone.

Scholastic, 60¢ (4–6)
Miss P's red rocks from Mars are on a ship that sinks. Information about deep-sea diving and atomic submarines is given before Miss P puts on skin-diving equipment and rescues her precious collection.

McSwigan, Marie *Snow Treasure* Illus. by the author.

Scholastic (Starline), 75¢ (4–6)
Based on a true incident, this is the story of Norwegian children who sledded twelve miles every other day for weeks past the Nazi soldiers who had invaded their country, with as much as 75 pounds of gold bullion on each sled. Eventually $9 million in gold reached the United States.

Marriott, Alice *The Black Stone Knife* Illus. by H. Weisa.

WSP (Archway), 60¢ (4–6)
Five Kiowa Indian boys travel south as far as Mexico following summer. They return home after two and a half years with an adopted brother and some black stone knives.

Martin, Patricia Miles *Calvin and the Cub Scouts* Illus. by Tom Hamil.

Scholastic, 60¢ (1–3)
Calvin loves the Cub Scouts but he is having great difficulty meeting the requirements for his bear badge. He finally achieves his goal, but in a most unpredictable and humorous manner.

MASON, MIRIAM E., ADAPTER   *Caroline and Her Kettle Named Maud*
Scholastic, 60¢   (3–6)
Caroline expects a gun as a going-away present when her family
leaves to brave the Michigan wilderness. The copper kettle she
receives instead is a disappointment until it helps to catch a wolf
when all the guns fail to do so.

MASON, MIRIAM E.   *The Middle Sister*
Scholastic, 60¢   (2–4)
Sarah Samantha is afraid of everything, including all the farm
animals. Uncle Romeo promises that when she makes an apple
dumpling from the apples on her own tree, he will give her his
lion's tooth and that it will make her brave. By the time Sarah has
protected her tree and its apples from the hazards of a trip to
Minnesota, winter, Indians, pigs, and grasshoppers, she is braver
in truth than she believes the tooth makes her.

MEADER, STEPHEN W.   *Bulldozer*   Illus. by Edwin Schmidt.
Harcourt (Voyager), 65¢   (6 up)
An optimistic account of a high school graduate who develops a
profitable business running a bulldozer. Lots of bulldozer mechan-
ics and 1951 prices.

MEADER, STEPHEN W.   *Who Rides in the Dark?*   Illus. by James
MacDonald.
Harcourt (Voyager), 75¢   (6 up)
Dan Drew, an orphan, becomes a stable boy at a New Hampshire
inn in the days of stagecoaches and highwaymen. Involved over
and over again with Cap'n Hairtrigger, the most famous of the
highwaymen, Dan is finally responsible for his capture.

MEADOWCROFT, ENID LA MONTE   *By Secret Railway*
Scholastic, 75¢   (5–7)
Although basically a story of the escape of a Negro slave from
Missouri to Illinois aided by a white boy, there are added sidelights
of the Republican convention in Chicago in 1860 and the Chicago
reaction to Lincoln's election.

MEADOWCROFT, ENID LA MONTE   *Silver for General Washington*
Scholastic, 75¢   (4–6)
Sent to a farm at Valley Forge to escape the British attack on
Philadelphia, Gil and Jen are there when General Washington and
his 11,000 starving, freezing men arrive. Gil and his cousin
go back to Philadelphia to sell the family silver to raise money
for the army. A detailed picture of the conditions of that winter.

MERRILL, JEAN *Pushcart War* Illus. by Ronnie Silbert.
Grosset (Tempo), 60¢ (5–7)
A delightful satire on world politics. Younger children will enjoy
the story about a war against trucks started by pushcart peddlers
who are being blamed for the congested traffic conditions in New
York City.

MILNE, A. A. *The House at Pooh Corner* Illus. by Ernest H.
Shepard.
Dell (Yearling), 75¢; Dutton, $1.25 (4–6)
A sequel to *Winnie-the-Pooh*. There are the same delightful
characters with one addition, Tigger, who leads his companions
into some new and exciting adventures.

MILNE, A. A. *Once On a Time* Illus. by S. Perl.
Avon (Camelot), 60¢ (4–6)
An original fairy tale with well-developed characters including
two kings, a princess, a scheming countess, and an enchanted
prince and a hero.

MILNE, A. A. *Winnie-The-Pooh* Illus. by Ernest H. Shepard.
Dell (Yearling), 75¢ (4–6)
Stories about the loveable bear Winnie-the-Pooh and his friends,
Christopher Robin, Owl, Eeyore, Kanga, Little Roo, Piglet, and
Rabbit.

MIRSKY, REBA PAEFF *Thirty-one Brothers and Sisters*
Dell (Yearling), 75¢ (4–8)
Everyday customs in a Zulu village do not permit girls to go on
elephant hunts, but Nomusa proves she is a worthy exception.

MONTGOMERY, L. M. *Anne of Green Gables*
Grosset (Tempo), 75¢ (6 up)
A red-headed, beauty-loving orphan, very imaginative and extremely talkative, is adopted by an old bachelor and his sister.
Anne boasts that she never makes the same mistake twice, to
which her foster mother replies, "I don't know as that's much
benefit when you're always making new ones."

MONTGOMERY, RUTHERFORD *El Blanco: The Legend of the White
Stallion* Illus. by G. Stevens.
Scholastic, 60¢ (4–6)
A legend is told in the mountains of Mexico about El Blanco whose
coming brought rain to the valley. Could such a horse be saved
from horse hunters in search of wild horses?

MONTGOMERY, RUTHERFORD *Kildee House* Illus. by Barbara Conney.

WSP (Archway), 75¢ (4–6)

Mr. Kildee built his home against a redwood tree in the middle of his hundred acres of land so he could be a hermit with nothing to do. His dream backfired, and he found himself foster father to 30 skunks, 25 racoons, and 2 warring teenagers.

MOREY, WALT *Gentle Ben* Illus. by J. Schoenherr.

Grosset (Tempo), 60¢; Scholastic, 75¢ (5–7)

Not every parent would consider a grown brown bear a suitable pet for his son, and Mark's parents take a lot of persuading before they let Mark have Ben. Later, when they decide Ben is too dangerous and send him away, everything seems to go wrong for them.

MOTT, MICHAEL *Master Entrick*

Dell (Yearling), 75¢ (4–6)

This adventure story is set in 18th century America during the French and Indian War. Robert Entrick is mysteriously kidnapped and forced to live a harsh life as bond servant to a rough settler. In the process he develops new self-reliance.

MURPHY, SHIRLEY ROUSSEAU *White Ghost Summer* Illus. by Barbara McGee.

Viking (Seafarer), 75¢ (4–6)

Moving into an old house by the sea proves exciting for Mel who sees a mysterious white horse through the early morning mists. Adventure abounds as she unravels the mystery of the horse and her fondest wish comes true.

NASH, MARY *Mrs. Coverlet's Magicians* Illus. by Garrett Price.

Scholastic, 60¢ (4–6)

The fun-loving Persever children have a rolicking Christmas when little brother Toad adopts a litter of kittens.

NESBIT, E. *Five Children and It* Illus. by H. R. Millar.

Penguin (Puffin), 75¢ (5–7)

Four children and a baby brother discover a weird-looking fairy creature who says it is a sand fairy and can grant wishes. Luckily, the effects of wishes don't last past sundown because every wish—whether for money, to be in a besieged castle, or to be bigger than the baker boy—turns out to be troublesome.

NESBIT, E. *The Story of the Treasure Seekers* Illus. by C. Leslie.

Penguin (Puffin), 75¢ (5–7)

The Bastable children try to recoup the family fortunes by digging for treasure, by finding a princess to marry, by rescuing an old man in dire peril, and by other romantic means, all equally unsuccessful.

NESBIT, E.   *The Wouldbegoods*

Penguin (Puffin), $1.25   (4–7)
Eight children can get into unbelievable messes, even if their intentions are good. For example, they see a friend's barge stranded in a dry lock of the canal so they open the lock, ruin an angling competition, and swamp the barge, causing it to lose its load.

NEWELL, HOPE   *Mary Ellis, Student Nurse*

Berkley, 50¢   (5–8)
Mary finds her second year of student nursing a real challenge and feels overwhelmed by the grave responsibilities placed upon her. But things seem a little brighter when she meets a certain young intern.

NIXON, JOAN LOWERY   *Mystery of the Secret Stowaway*   Illus. by Mort Junstler.

Scholastic, 60¢   (4–6)
Joe stows away on an ocean liner seeking adventure and fun, but what he finds is an intriguing mystery as well as a family who takes him under their wing.

NOLAN, JEANNETTE COVER   *The Victory Drum*   Illus. by L. F. Bjorklund.

WSP (Archway), 50¢   (5–7)
Benny, age 12, is too young to enlist in George Rogers Clark's troop as a soldier, but he goes along as a drummer boy when the Americans march from Kaskaskia to Vincennes and recapture the fort. The 240-mile trip is made during the most rainey February in memory, across the Drowned Lands with hostile Miami Indians on the prowl.

NORRIS, FAITH, AND LUMN, P.   *Kim of Korea*   Illus. by Kurt Wiese.

WSP (Archway), 60¢   (5–7)
After an American soldier promises that he will adopt him and take him to the United States, Kim is separated from his new foster father and takes a roundabout journey from Seoul to Inchon to find him. Along the way he encounters an escaped criminal and travels with an acrobatic troop and with an old Japanese gentlemen.

NORTON, MARY *The Borrowers* Illus. by Beth and Jo Krush.
Harcourt (Voyager), 75¢ (4–6)
The Borrowers—those little people who live in odd hiding places in a house and borrow things such as thimbles, spools, postage stamps, pins, and the like—live in fear of being seen. Arriety is seen by a boy and soon learns that her parents' fears are well founded.

OAKES, VANYA *Hawaiian Treasure* Illus. by I. Kashiwage.
WSP (Archway), 60¢ (5–7)
Visiting from the mainland, Tom makes friends with several native Hawaiians of Hawaiian, Japanese, and Chinese extraction and, joining their Scout troop, visits their families, goes on a wild pig hunt, takes part in an archeological expedition, and helps a rescue mission during a volcanic eruption.

OAKES, VANYA *Willy Wong: American* Illus. by W. Yak.
WSP (Archway), 50¢ (5–7)
Willy lives in two worlds—Chinese at home and American at school. His Chinese life emphasizes and approves his artistic talents, but the American side seems to demand proficiency in baseball. The Chinese contributions to building the transcontinental railroad a century ago help Willy reconcile his two worlds.

O'CONNOR, PATRICK *The Black Tiger*
Berkley, 50¢ (5–8)
In this fast-paced sports story, everyone believes the Black Tiger is a jinxed racing car. But young Woody Hartford, filled with pride and a desire to win, decides this is the car he must race.

OFFIT, SIDNEY *Soupbone* Illus. by Paul Galdone.
WSP (Archway), 50¢ (4–6)
Soupbone McDexter, world famous pitcher, is Joe's hero. So, wanting Soupbone and his team to win the season's pennant, Joe and his friends concoct a secret potion that causes some hilarious happenings at game time.

O'HARA, MARY *My Friend Flicka*
Dell (Laurel-Leaf), 60¢ (6 up)
An adult book, adopted by children. The McLaughlin ranch is not particularly successful, and Ken feels very alienated from his father and continually guilty because his daydreams and foolish acts irritate his father and cost him money. Finally granted permission to have a colt, he chooses Flicka, granddaughter of a albino whose wild blood has tainted the McLaughlin strain.

O'HARA, MARY   *Thunderhead*

Dell (Laurel-Leaf), 60¢   (6 up)
Nell McLaughlin, Ken's mother, is the central character in this
sequel to *My Friend Flicka,* and marital discord is the central
theme, although it also is the story of Thunderhead, Flicka's colt, a
throwback to his albino ancestor.

OLDS, HELEN DIEHL   *Detour for Meg*

WSP (Archway), 50¢   (6 up)
A not very serious automobile accident has far-reaching consequences. Robert loses the notebook that meant his scholarship for
college, and Meg, terrified of driving, finds herself in a driver's
education course. There is also the mystery of two hit-and-run
accidents.

ORTON, HELEN FULLER   *Mystery in the Pirate Oak*

Scholastic, 50¢   (3–4)
The pirate oak conceals several mysteries that attract children and
adults alike—pirate treasure buried at the roots and a valuable
silver box hidden some place among the branches. Chad and Ellie
plan to solve the mysteries until the son of the new owner of the
tree forbids them to trespass.

PARKER, RICHARD   *M For Mischief*   Illus. by Carol Wilde.

Scholastic, 50¢   (2–4)
The odd stove in the summer house has a dial on the front: 0 for
ordinary, M for mischief. The cookbook that accompanies the
stove allows the children to cook eggs that make them invisible
and cookies that turn people into domestic animals.

PARKINSON, ETHELYN M.   *Double Trouble for Rupert*   Illus. by
Mary Stevens.

Scholastic, 50¢   (4–6)
Twelve-year-old Rupert and his pals have some hilarious adventures at school and at home. Contributing to their problems are a
couple of classmates who happen to be girls.

PHIPSON, JOAN   *The Family Conspiracy*   Illus. by M. Horder.

Harcourt (Voyager), 65¢   (5–7)
Money is scarce in New South Wales, and ways for children to
make money are even scarcer. The Barker children decide to earn
money for their mother's operation and to keep their plans secret.
But Belinda causes more expense by needing glasses for strained
eyes, Robbie is nearley killed in a deserted gold mine, and Lorna
hurts her parents by staying at a friend's house during vacation.

POE, EDGAR ALLAN *Ten Great Mysteries* Edited and introduction by Groff Conklin. Illus. by Irv Docktor.

Scholastic, 60¢ (6 up)

Among more familiar stories of Poe presented here are "The Pit and the Pendulum" and "The Tell-Tale Heart."

PYLE, HOWARD *Men of Iron*

Scholastic, 60¢ (6 up)

Noble knighthood, plus a good look at what went on behind the scenes. Myles Falworth is trained as a knight and learns that a large number of people expect him to defeat the Earl of Alban, confidante of King Henry IV, in single combat to clear his father of a charge of treason.

PYLE, HOWARD *Otto of the Silver Hand* Illus. by the author.

Dover, $1.75 (6 up)

A simple, poignant story of revenge and what constituted true manhood in the days of knights.

RAWLINGS, MARJORIE KINNAN *The Yearling*

Scribner, $2.45 (6 up)

Young Jody Baxter lived a lonely life in the scrub forest of Florida. The companionship he found in an orphan fawn was lost when he had to give it up.

REESE, JOHN *Big Mutt* Illus. by Rod Ruth.

WSP (Archway), 60¢ (5–7)

Big Mutt—raised in New York City and abandoned by his owners in the Badlands of North Dakota on the eve of one of the worst winters in history—kills sheep to keep alive. Pursued by the sheepmen of the region, he is saved by a boy who feels that the dog can be tamed.

REYNOLDS, BARBARA LEONARD *Emily San*

Scholastic, 60¢ (4–6)

Americans in Rainbow Village in Japan are like giraffes—afraid to leave the familiar and find out what Japan is like. Emily Masters and her family lead some of them into another world.

RINKOFF, BARBARA *Elbert, The Mind Reader* Illus. by Paul Galdone.

Scholastic, 60¢ (3–5)

Few children have the incentive to brush their teeth that Elbert has. His new filling acts as a radio and, when brushed very hard, enables him to read minds. A quarterback too small to play football can still be valuable if he's quick to figure out his opponents' plays.

ROBERTSON, KEITH *Henry Reed, Inc.* Illus. by Robert McCloskey.
Grosset (Tempo), 60¢ (4–6)
Henry Reed, son of an American diplomat, spends his first summer
in his native land with his aunt and uncle in Princeton, New
Jersey. In their efforts to demonstrate free enterprise, Henry and
his partner Midge "take objects which are ordinarily considered
free and sell them." Complications arise from an escaped white
rabbit, a cantankerous neighbor, and a stray beagle.

ROBERTSON, KEITH *Henry Reed's Baby-sitting Service*
Grosset (Tempo), 60¢ (4–6)
Henry and Midge open a baby-sitting service and cope with the
disappearances of one of their clients, of a house trailer, and of the
water in a swimming pool and with the continual appearances at
the wrong times of a red MG driven by either one of the unpleasant
neighbor twins.

ROBERTSON, KEITH *Henry Reed's Journey*
Grosset (Tempo), 60¢ (4–6)
Henry travels across America by car with Midge and her parents.
As usual, Henry's complete lack of a sense of humor merely
emphasizes the ridiculous situations the children get themselves
into—starting a gold rush, getting adopted by an Indian tribe, and
trying to buy fireworks.

ROUNDS, GLEN *The Blind Colt*
Scholastic, 60¢ (4–6)
The sounds, smells, and feel of things dominate this account of the
first year in the life of a blind range colt, who survived very well
despite the dire predictions of Uncle Torwal that he would be
"wolf et."

RUSHMORE, HELEN *Cowboy Joe of the Circle S* Illus. by P. Burchard.
Harcourt (Voyager), 75¢ (3–5)
When his misadventures on the ranch first saddle him with names
like Dude and Dogie, Joe tries to earn a good cowboy name. He
succeeds and becomes Chip (off the old block) when he puts out a
forest fire.

RUSHMORE, HELEN *Ghost Cat* Illus. by Reisie Lonette.
Scholastic, 60¢ (3–5)
Glory doesn't believe all the ghost stories the grown-ups tell. She
sets out to prove there are no haunted houses but discovers some
spooky surprises along the way.

SACHS, MARILYN   *Amy and Laura*
Scholastic, 60¢ (4–6)
Mother is back from the hospital, and Laura, heartbroken, finds things are worse instead of better. Her close relationship with her mother seems to be destroyed, and she finds it hard never to tell her any problems to keep her from worrying. Amy gets along just fine.

SACHS, MARILYN   *Amy Moves In*   Illus. by Mac Conner.
Scholastic, 75¢ (4–6)
Amy's family moves into a new apartment in a strange neighborhood. She makes new friends who are, in the eyes of her family, the wrong ones. Then her mother is badly hurt in an automobile accident, and Amy's problems, especially that of having a vivid imagination (otherwise known as lying), increase.

SACHS, MARILYN   *Veronica Ganz*   Illus. by Louis Ganzman.
WSP (Archway), 60¢ (5–6)
A realistic story of a tomboy and how she plans to get even with Peter, the only fellow from school who has outsmarted her. Veronica's family life and divorced parents are tactfully introduced.

SAINT-EXUPERY, ANTOINE DE   *The Little Prince*
Harcourt (Voyager), 75¢ (6 up)
The generation gap is poetically described in a book written 25 years before the term existed. The Little Prince, on his way to Earth, visits various planetoids and comes away from each feeling that "Grown-ups are certainly very, very odd," in their sense of values. Translated from the French.

ST. JOHN, WYLLY FOLK   *The Secrets of Hidden Creek*   Illus. by Paul Galdone.
Viking (Seafarer), 65¢ (4–6)
A stolen collection of 59 gold pieces, a lost treasury of Confederate gold, a haunted house, and a thief's son! The summer turned out to be not dull at all for the Dodd children visiting their grandparents.

SALTEN, FELIX   *Bambi*
Grosset (Tempo), 60¢ (5 up)
A young deer grows to maturity and in so doing learns to respect an old stag and to fear man.

SAWYER, RUTH   *Roller Skates*   Illus. by V. Angelo.
Dell (Yearling), 95¢ (6 up)
One year of freedom as a temporary orphan is well spent by

Lucinda, age 10. With a catholic taste in friends, she borrows the baby from upstairs, helps the Italian boy at the fruit stand get rid of some thieving bullies, and joyfully makes the acquaintance of Shakespeare. Almost the entire book is as joyful as Lucinda skating full speed through the streets of New York. Awarded the Newbery Medal in 1937.

SCOTT, SIR WALTER *Ivanhoe*
Airmont, 75¢; Dell (Laurel), 75¢; Harper, 85¢; Macmillan (Collier),
    95¢; NAL (Signet), 75¢; WSP, 60¢; Scholastic, 75¢ (6 up)
Blonde Rowena, brunette Rebecca, and a kingdom are at stake. The heroes, all very heroic, are almost all in disguise. The villains are thoroughly villainous, and there are knights, besieged castles, and tournaments.

SENJE, SIGURD *Escape*
                                              Harcourt (Voyager), 60¢ (6 up)
Ill and near death, an artistic Russian prisoner of war, made a scapegoat by a German camp commander, is rescued by the Norwegian underground and sent, in slow stages, to Sweden. Translated from the Norwegian.

SEREDY, KATE *The Good Master*
                                                    Dell (Yearling), 75¢ (5–7)
"She is the most impossible, incredible, disobedient, headstrong little imp. She needs a strong hand." Cousin Kate from Budapest finds a strong hand on the Hungarian ranch of her uncle.

SEWELL, ANNA *Black Beauty*
                                                    Airmont, 50¢; Dell, 60¢;
        Penguin (Puffin), 95¢; Scholastic (Starline), 60¢ (4–6)
Black Beauty describes her life as a horse in 19th century England, detailing also many unhappy and unpleasant happenings in the lives of many acquaintances.

SHARP, MARGERY *Miss Bianca* Illus. by G. Williams.
                                                        Berkley, 75¢ (4–6)
Mice don't particularly like little girls, who are all too likely to have kittens, but Miss Bianca goes off to rescue an orphan kidnapped by the cruel grand duchess. And Bernard rescues Miss Bianca.

SHARP, MARGERY *The Rescuers* Illus. by G. Williams.
                                                        Berkley 75¢ (4–6)
A beautiful, pampered, pet white mouse, Miss Bianca, yields to

cupid's lures and joins a prisoners' aid society rescue team to free a Norwegian poet from the Black Castle.

SHARP, MARGERY *The Turret* Illus. by G. Williams.

Berkley, 75¢ (4–6)

Mandrake, steward of the grand duchess, is imprisoned in the turret. Only Miss Bianca, an adventuresome white mouse, has faith that he has reformed and is worth saving.

SHOTWELL, LOUISA R. *Roosevelt Grady* Illus. by Peter Burchard.

Grosset (Tempo), 60¢; Scholastic (Starline), 60¢ (4–6)

The illustrations tell that these migrant workers, following the crops of the truck farmers, are black. Young Roosevelt has a little desire and a big desire: He wants to know what to do with the leftover if you're "putting into" and it doesn't come out even, and he wants a permanent home.

SILVERBERG, ROBERT *Lost Race of Mars* Illus. by Leonard Kessler.

Scholastic, 60¢ (4–6)

In this exciting science fiction story, the year is 2017, and a scientist and his children travel to Mars in search of the Old Martian race.

SIMON, SHIRLEY *Best Friend* Illus. by R. Lonette.

WSP (Archway), 60¢ (5–7)

Jenny is completely lost when her best friend, Dot, moves to a nearby apartment hotel and makes new friends. But when Dot again wants to be her best friend again, Jenny's own experiences and those of her older sister and her unorthodox grandmother make her realize that she doesn't want just one best friend.

SKINNER, CONSTANCE LINDSAY *Becky Landers*

Macmillan (Collier), 79¢ (6 up)

Fifteen-year-old Becky is as good with a gun as a boy—something very important on the Kentucky frontier during the Revolution. She also has good friends—Daniel Boone, Simon Kenton, George Rogers Clark, and Dangiaux de Quindre, French leader of the Indians fighting for the British.

SLEPIAN, JAN AND SEIDLER, ANN *The Hungry Thing* Illus. by Richard E. Martin.

Scholastic, 75¢ (3–4)

A hungry monster comes to a town and wants all sorts of exotic things to eat. Prose and poetry tell what the people fed him. The colorful illustrations add to the humor of the story.

SMITH, DODIE   *One Hundred and One Dalmatians*
Avon (Camelot), 75¢   (5–6)
Cruella de Vil kidnaps the 15 pups belonging to Pongo and Missis, and the devoted parents set off to rescue them, gathering information through the Twilight Barking System that covers all dogdom.

SNYDER, ZILPHA KEATLEY   *The Velvet Room*   Illus. by Alton Raible.
Scholastic, 75¢   (4–7)
A migrant worker and his family obtain work on a California ranch during the Depression. Robin escapes the dreariness of her life when she discovers a special reading nook in a closed-up house on the ranch. In solving the mystery in the ranch owner's family, she also finds direction for her own life.

SOBOL, DONALD J.   *Encyclopedia Brown*
Scholastic (Starline), 50¢   (4–6)
Short mysteries provide all the clues that the boy detective has and give the reader a chance to solve them too.

SOBOL, DONALD J.   *Encyclopedia Brown Gets His Man*
Scholastic (Starline), 50¢   (4–6)
Encyclopedia solves mysteries caused by the neighborhood bully and adult problems for his father, the police chief. The reader can also try his skill.

SOBOL, DONALD J.   *Encyclopedia Brown Strikes Again*
Scholastic, 50¢   (4–6)
Further adventures of the boy detective.

SOBOL, DONALD J.   *Secret Agents Four*   Illus. by Leonard Shortall.
Scholastic, 60¢   (4–6)
When one wants to be a secret agent, it helps to have a father working for Mongoose (the American agency dedicated to the overthrow of Cobra, the enemy organization), a girl friend who knows judo, and a boy friend who invents incredible machines.

SOUTHALL, IVAN   *Hills End*   Illus. by J. Phillips.
WSP (Archway), 60¢   (6 up)
After a cyclone, seven children and their teacher are isolated in their ruined community without electricity or drinking water. Separated from their teacher, the children struggle to provide themselves with food and shelter, harried by a mean bull and near nervous exhaustion from their fears and lack of leadership.

SPEEVACK, YETTA   *The Spider Plant*   Illus. by W. Watson.
WSP (Archway), 50¢   (5–7)
At first the spider plant was just something green in the dark, sunless apartment. But when Carmen and her family moved into a new apartment, it helped the Puerto Rican girl make new friends and even helped her brother Pedro to be happier in New York.

SPERRY, ARMSTRONG   *Call It Courage*
Scholastic, 50¢   (4–6)
A tale of fear overcome. What could be worse for a Polynesian boy, the son of a chief, than to be afraid of the sea? Mafatu sets out alone in an outrigger canoe to prove to himself and others that he is not a coward, even if he is afraid. Awarded the Newbery Medal in 1941.

SPYKMAN, E. C.   *Terrible, Horrible Edie*
Harcourt (Voyager), 75¢   (5–7)
Aunt Charlotte said that if Mr. Parker could just keep all the Cares children alive for the summer, it would exceed her greatest expectations. Edie makes the job difficult, running away to camp on the island, sailing in impossible weather, and trying to capture a jewel thief.

SPYRI, JOHANNA   *Heidi*   Illus. by John Ferni.
Airmont, 50¢; Scholastic (Starline), 75¢   (5 up)
It is hoped that the television and motion picture presentations of this children's classic haven't discouraged their viewers, for the book is a much happier story than the subsequent versions. Heidi is happier with her grandfather, Klara is happier with Heidi, and Peter's grandmother is happier for the rest of her life.

STAFFORD, JEAN   *Elephi, The Cat with the High IQ*   Illus. by Eric Blegvad.
Dell (Yearling), 65¢   (3–5)
Mr. Cuckoo tells the police, "There's a strange car in my apartment." The Cuckoos knew that Elephi is smart enough to steal a car, but he has stolen it because he wanted something to play with.

STAHL, BEN   *Blackbeard's Ghost*   Illus. by the author.
Scholastic (Starline), 60¢   (5 up)
Blackbeard's ghost objected to the demolition of his old tavern to make way for a modern gas station. Although only a few privileged people—and J. D. and Hank didn't consider themselves privileged exactly—could see him, everyone could feel the ghost's displeasure.

STEELE, WILLIAM O.   *The Buffalo Knife* Illus. by Paul Galdone.
Harcourt (Voyager), 65¢   (4–7)
Andy can't understand why Isaac would rather stay in town than
take the raft trip down the Tennessee, braving the Chickamaugas
and the rapids, to a new settlement.

STEELE, WILLIAM O.   *The Perilous Road* Illus. by Paul Galdone.
Harcourt (Voyager), 75¢   (5–7)
Eleven-year-old Chris Babson wages a one-man war against the
Union army.

STERLING, DOROTHY   *Mary Jane*
Scholastic, 75¢   (5–7)
An intimate story of the feelings of a black girl who is one of the
first small group of blacks attending a formerly all white high
school. Mary Jane plans to approach the problem as if she were an
ambassador to a foreign country. She finds it much more difficult
than she ever dreamed.

STERLING, DOROTHY   *Mystery of the Empty House*
Scholastic, 60¢   (4–6)
The Paine house, which has been in the family since Revolution-
ary times, is going to be sold for taxes. With the help of a college
student, the Paine boys and their neighbors locate the lost treasure, and Pat and Barbara break the code in which the letters are
written and prove their value. Original title was *Secret of the Old
Post Box.*

STERLING, DOROTHY   *The Silver Spoon Mystery*
Scholastic, 60¢   (4–6)
The girls' neighborhood newspaper reports the theft of the silver
spoons before it happens. This sequence confuses the girls, the
police, and the real thief.

STERNE, EMMA GELDERS   *The Long Black Schooner*
Scholastic, 75¢   (5–7)
A group of Africans, sold into slavery but led by a strong, intelligent leader, take over the ship carrying them to a Cuban planta-
tion and try to sail it back to Africa. Eventually the American
courts decide on the legality of murder, mutiny, and their slavery.

STEVENSON, ROBERT LOUIS   *Black Arrow: A Tale of the Two Roses*
Airmont, 50¢; Dell (Laurel-Leaf), 45¢;
Lancer, 60¢; Scholastic, 60¢   (6 up)
England may be fighting the War of the Roses, but Dick Shelton

has little time for politics. He has to avenge his father's death and rescue his true love, and for those tasks the band of the Black Arrow is more help than lords and dukes.

STEVENSON, ROBERT LOUIS *Kidnapped*
Airmont, 50¢; Dell (Laurel-Leaf), 45¢; NAL (Signet), 50¢; Pyramid, 50¢; WSP (Archway), 75¢; Scholastic, 75¢ (6 up)
David Balfour chooses his friends poorly. His uncle tries to murder him; the ship's captain tries to murder him; and Alan Breck Steward, with a price on his head, gets a price put on David's head. The scene is Scotland in 1751, and the action involves a chase through the length of Scotland.

STEVENSON, ROBERT LOUIS *Treasure Island*
Airmont, 50¢; Dell (Laurel-Leaf), 45¢; NAL(Signet), 50¢; Penguin (Puffin), 65¢; Scholastic, 75¢ (6 up)
It's an unlucky day for pirates when Jim Hawkins becomes involved in their treasure hunt. He finds the treasure map first, overhears their treacherous plans of murder, steals their ship, and even steals their captain.

STOLZ, MARY *The Bully of Barkham Street* Illus. by Leonard Shortall.
Dell (Yearling), 75¢ (4–6)
What makes a bully? Why would the son of an average middle-class family become a rude, disrespectful, lying, bullying loner? The background is given from Martin Hastings' own point of view.

STOLZ, MARY *The Dog on Barkham Street* Illus. by Leonard Shortall.
Dell (Yearling), 75¢ (4–6)
Edward Frost has two problems—he wants a dog, and he is the victim of the bully next door—Martin Hastings. He can't have a dog until he shows he is responsible, but when his hobo uncle comes along, Edward wonders what is so desirable about responsibility.

STONE, EUGENIA *Page Boy of Camelot* Illus. by Mort Kunstler.
Scholastic, 60¢ (4–6)
Tor, son of a cowherd, is allowed to work at Camelot, but his disobedience causes him to be moved from the kitchen, to the falconer, to the armorer, and back to his home. Given a second chance, he becomes page to Sir Galahad. Original title was *Page Boy for King Arthur*.

STORR, CATHERINE *Marianne Dreams*

Penguin (Puffin), 95¢ (4–6)

A young girl who finds a pencil in an old workbox suddenly begins to dream about everything she draws with it.

SUTCLIFF, ROSEMARY *Outcast*

Dell (Laurel-Leaf), 50¢ (6 up)

Roman Britain, the city of Rome, and ancient ships are dramatically portrayed as Beric, exiled by his British tribe, becomes a house slave in Rome and then a galley slave, before he finds a place for himself in the world of freemen.

SWIFT, JONATHAN *Gulliver's Travels*

Airmont, 50¢; Dell, 50¢; Macmillan (Collier), 65¢;
NAL (Signet), 50¢; WSP, 45¢ (6 up)

Lemuel Gulliver is imprisoned among the Lilliputians, to whom he is a giant, and among the Brobdingnagians, who are giants to him, and then visits other odd peoples.

TAYLOR, SYDNEY *All-of-a-Kind Family* Illus. by Helen John.

Dell (Yearling), 65¢ (3–5)

An episodic but engaging story of a Jewish family with five daughters living on New York's Lower East Side in 1912. The celebration of Jewish holidays plays a major part in their lives.

TAYLOR, SYDNEY *All-of-a-Kind Family Uptown* Illus. by Mary Stevens.

Dell (Yearling), 65¢ (3–5)

The family has moved out of its all Jewish neighborhood. Mama goes to the hospital, and the girls manage the house, even with visitors. Ella's boyfriend goes into the army, and Hymen and Lenn have a baby.

TAYLOR, SYDNEY *More All-of-a-Kind Family* Illus. by Mary Stevens.

Dell (Yearling), 65¢ (3–5)

The second book in the series. Romance enters the lives of Uncle Hyman and Ella. Baby Charlie is heartbroken when his mother frowns at him, and Henny's friend Fanny gets spanked instead of Henny.

THACKERAY, W. M. *The Rose and the Ring*

Penguin (Puffin), 65¢ (4–7)

A ring and a rose with the power to make their owners loved wreak havoc with the romantic and governmental affairs of two nations, both with usurpers on the thrones.

TOMERLIN, JOHN   *The Magnificent Jalopy*
Dutton, $1.25   (5–8)
Purchase and renovation of the Phantom, a 1930 Packard car, brings excitement to a boring summer for three teenagers. Their real adventures begin when they sign up for a 1000-mile road rally.

TRAVERS, P. L.   *I Go By Sea, I Go By Land*
Dell (Yearling), 65¢   (4–6)
Based on a real diary, this is this diary of Sabrina Lind, age 11, who, with her brother, is sent to America from England to escape the German bombs of World War II. A touching portrayal of children excited by new adventures but torn by love and fear for the family and home from which they are separated.

TREECE, HENRY   *Splintered Sword*   Illus. by C. Keeping.
Avon (Camelot), 60¢   (6 up)
Heir to a berserker's battered sword, Runolf sets out to help Prince Nial get a kingdom, unable to realize that Nial is a rogue rather than royalty.

TUNIS, JOHN R.   *The Kid Comes Back*
Scholastic (Starline), 75¢   (6 up)
The kid is in the army, crashes behind enemy lines, and is rescued by a marquis. Returning to baseball, he is severely hampered in regaining his place on the team by a wartime back injury.

TURNGREN, ANNETTE   *Mystery Clouds the Canyon*
Berkley, 50¢   (7–8)
This fast-paced mystery has its brilliant setting in the California mountains. Cindy Harrow, her brother, and a friend travel there to look for her brother's roommate and discover mystery and adventure at every turn.

TWAIN, MARK   *The Prince and the Pauper*
Airmont, 50¢; Macmillan (Collier), 95¢   (6 up)
Tom Canty, born in a hovel, and Edward Tudor, who becomes Edward VI, look as alike as identical twins. Allowed to exchange places in life for a short time, each is astonished and a little horrified by the widely contrasting way of life of the other.

ULLMAN, JAMES RAMSEY   *Banner in the Sky*   Illus. by Kurt Wiese.
WSP (Archway), 60¢   (6 up)
The names are strange, but the face of the mountain is familiar. This suspenseful, detailed account of the successful ascent of an "unclimbable" Swiss alp owes something to the true story of the conquering of the Matterhorn.

VAN DER VEER, JUDY   *Hold the Rein Free*   Illus. by Pers Crowell.
Scholastic, 75¢   (4–6)
A Mexican boy and a city-bred girl steal a filly about to foal and
hide her in a forgotten corral because the thoroughbred's owner
has decreed that the foal is to be killed as soon as it is born. The
children have an exciting time caring for the mare and her colt as
a variety of people begin to suspect that they know more than they
are telling.

VERNE, JULES   *Around the World in 80 Days*
Scholastic, 60¢   (6 up)
Phileas Fogg not only wins his bet by going around the world in 80
days in the year 1872, but he does so hampered by the actions of a
detective following him, who believes Fogg to be a thief, and by a
newly acquired fiancée.

VERNE, JULES   *From the Earth to the Moon*
Scholastic, 60¢   (6 up)
Several members of the gun club, bored by the lack of a war to
utilize their talents, decide to shoot a projectile to the moon. When
their plans are complete, the empty sphere becomes a cone containing three passengers. Verne's gift of prophesy is awe-inspiring
to readers of the Apollo age.

VERNE, JULES   *The Mysterious Island*
Airmont, 60¢; Scholastic, 75¢   (6 up)
Cyrus Harding is the man to have with you if you plan to be
shipwrecked with only your clothes, a watch, and a dog as resour-
ces. Verne's five adventurers succeed admirably, manufacturing
nitroglycerin and glass and smelting iron, in addition to providing
themselves with the more common necessities.

VERNE, JULES   *20,000 Leagues Under the Sea*
Airmont, 50¢;   Bantam (Pathfinder), 75¢;
WSP (Archway), 95¢; Scholastic, 75¢   (6 up)
M. Aronnax, his servant, and an American harpooner become
uninvited guests on Captain Nemo's electrically driven sub-
marine. Captain Nemo has invented an aqua-lung, and the men
enjoy marine biology in detail, walk on sunken Atlantis, go
through a tunnel under the Isthmus of Suez, almost get frozen in
at the South Pole, and travel 20,000 leagues while underwater.

VINTON, IRIS   *Boy on the Mayflower*   Illus. by John Nielsen.
Scholastic (Starline), 50¢   (3–5)
A fictional account of the crossing of the *Mayflower*. A picture of a
cross-section of the ship will be useful for history projects.

WALDEN, AMELIA ELIZABETH   *My Sister Mike*

Berkley, 50¢   (6–8)
Mike, a tomboy, was more interested in playing basketball than
dating, but her ideas suddenly changed when she discovered how
handsome the captain of the boys' team was.

WEBER, LENORA MATTINGLY   *Don't Call Me Katie Rose*

Berkley, 50¢   (5–8)
Longing to be glamorous, Katie Rose wants to forget she is part of
a large family and tries to act sophisticated, but circumstances
keep reminding Katie of her responsibilities.

WEBSTER, JEAN   *Daddy-Long-Legs*

Grosset (Tempo), 60¢   (6 up)
The letters from a naive orphan sent to college by a trustee of the
orphanage offer humor, romance, and a little mystery.

WHITE, ANNE H.   *Junket: The Dog Who Liked Everything Just
So*   Illus. by Robert McCloskey.

Viking (Seafarer), 75¢   (5–8)
When the city-bred McDonegals buy the farm where Junket lives,
he decides to teach them all about farm life. The illustrations
match the warm, humorous story.

WHITE, E. B.   *Charlotte's Web*   Illus. by Garth Williams.

Dell (Yearling), 95¢   (3–5)
Charlotte, a spider, spells out words in her web to save Wilbur, the
pig, from slaughter. The first words are "Some pig," and Mrs.
Zuckerman thinks it's really "Some spider," but the rest of the
humans are gullible enough to believe that Wilbur is responsible
for the miracle.

WHITE, E. B.   *Stuart Little*   Illus. by Garth Williams.

Dell (Yearling), 75¢   (3–5)
Stuart, the second son of the Little family, looks just like a mouse.
His size is an advantage when he wants to sail a toy boat on a
Central Park pond, but a disadvantage when he is picked up with
the garbage. After Margalo, a brown bird, leaves the Little house-
hold, Stuart starts out to find her.

WILLIAMS, URSULA MORAY   *The Moonball*   Illus. by Jane Paton.

Scholastic, 60¢   (4–6)
A mysterious furry ball with magical powers is found by a group of
children. The real adventure begins when it is taken away by a
professor for scientific study.

Williamson, Jack *Trapped in Space* Illus. by Robert Amundsen.
Scholastic, 60¢ (5–7)
Jeff's brother Ben, pilot of a space ship, is trapped by alien
creatures in this science fiction thriller. Jeff attempts a rescue but
finds himself ensnared in the same mysterious web.

Woolley, Catherine *A Room For Cathy*
Scholastic, 60¢ (4–6)
After considerable time and some sacrifice, Cathy finally gets a
beautiful room of her own, only to have to give it up when the
family is forced to rent rooms in their large house.

Worline, Bonnie *The Children Who Stayed Alone*
Scholastic, 60¢ (4–6)
Homesteaders on the Kansas prairie often lived in sod houses, and
Phoebe Dawson liked her home. Even though she didn't want
anything to change, she couldn't help maturing when she was left
in charge of her six brothers and sisters, made friends with the
Indians, worked in the home of settlers from Virginia, and helped
her family settle in their new frame house. Original title was *Sod
House Adventure.*

Wyndham, Lee *On Your Toes, Susie!* Illus. by Jane Miller.
Scholastic, 60¢ (4–6)
After three years of ballet lessons, Susie is finally ready for toe
dancing. But most of her pleasure is destroyed by the rivalry of a
visiting French ballet student who seems to take over Susie's place
in class as star pupil.

Wyss, Johann *The Swiss Family Robinson*
Airmont, 60¢; Dell (Laurel-Leaf), 50¢; Scholastic, 75¢ (5–7)
Parents and four sons are shipwrecked on a tropic isle and build an
extremely adequate home with the aid of much salvaged material.
Unlike most castaways, when discovered they decide to remain.

Young, Bob and Jan *Across the Tracks*
WSP (Archway), 60¢ (7 up)
This sensitive story of a popular high school girl who can't forget
her Mexican heritage helps to shed light on a current and agoniz-
ing problem.

Young, Miriam *The Dollar Horse* Illus. by William M. Hutchin-
son.
Scholastic, 60¢ (4–5)
What can a little boy do with one dollar? With imagination and

ambition, Keery works miracles with his birthday dollar and gets his real heart's desire.

YOUNG, MIRIAM *The Secret of Stone House Farm* Illus. by William M. Hutchinson.

Harcourt (Voyager), 60¢ (4–6)

The new people at Stone House Farm were to be avoided. They were different; they were circus people, and besides, they had some sort of secret. What attracts children more than a combination of circuses and secrets? Marcy and Lee have a thoroughly enjoyable summer involved with both.

NONFICTION

Animals and Pets

ADAMSON, JOY *Born Free*
Bantam (Pathfinder), 75¢ (5 up)
A game warden in Kenya and his wife adopt an orphaned lion cub, Elsa, rear her as a family pet, teach her to fend for herself, and release her when she is grown. Photographs.

ADAMSON, JOY *Living Free*
Bantam (Pathfinder), 75¢ (5 up)
Elsa, the lioness, raises her three cubs in the African bush with the help of the author and her husband. Well illustrated with photos.

BALCH, GLENN *The Book of Horses*
Scholastic, 60¢ (4–6)
This is illustrated with pictures of beautiful horses. It tells about different kinds of horses, important breeds, eastern and western riding, and how and where to ride and how to care for a horse.

BUCK, MARGARET WARING *Pets from the Pond* Illus. by the author.
Abingdon, $1.75 (4–6)
Included in this detailed book are instructions for making and maintaining an aquarium. The book also explains where to locate appropriate plants and animals and the necessary care to give them.

BUCK, MARGARET WARING *Small Pets from Woods and Fields*
Illus. by the author.

Abingdon, $1.75 (4–6)

This book will help boys and girls understand and observe the
habits of familiar woods creatures such as toads, snakes, and
butterflies—and gives instructions for housing, feeding, and caring for them.

COMPERE, MICHIE *Dolphins!* Illus. by Irma Wilde.

Scholastic (Starline), 50¢ (K–3)

The author tells how dolphins breathe, see, hear, sleep, and bring
up their families.

CRAIG, M. JEAN *Dinosaurs and More Dinosaurs* Illus. by George
Solonevich.

Scholastic, 75¢ (1–4)

Information on forty-six dinosaurs, well illustrated and indexed.

DARBY, GENE *What Is a Frog?* Illus. by Lucy and John Hawkinson.

Scholastic, 50¢ (K–2)

The metamorphosis from tadpole to frog is simply presented with
general information about the habits of these animals. Peculiari-
ties of certain kinds of frogs are also given.

GARELICK, MAY *What's Inside? The Story of an Egg that Hatched*
Photos by Rena Jakobsen.

Scholastic, 60¢ (K–2)

Excellent photographs capture the process of the birth of a chick.

GARELICK, MAY *Where Does the Butterfly Go When It Rains* Illus.
by Leonard Weisgard.

Scholastic, 60¢ (K–2)

A child knows how many animals find shelter from the rain, but
not how the butterfly does.

GEIS, DARLENE *How and Why Wonder Book of Dinosaurs* Illus. by
K. Shannon.

Wonder, 69¢ (3–5)

What do you want to know about dinosaurs? This book has the
answers.

HOGNER, DOROTHY *Odd Pets,* abridged ed. Photos by Lilo Hess.

Scholastic, 60¢ (4–7)

Tells how to care for animals that are not native to a domestic
environment.

KEEN, MARTIN L. *How and Why Wonder Book of Prehistoric Mammals* Illus. by J. Hall.

> Wonder, 69¢ (3–5)

Information about prehistoric mammals in a question-and-answer format.

KEEN, MARTIN L. *How and Why Wonder Book of Wild Animals* Illus. by W. Ferguson.

> Wonder, 69¢ (3–5)

Questions ranging from "What is a carnivore?" to "What animals can die of fright?" are answered about both common and uncommon wild animals.

MOODY, RALPH *Come On, Seabiscuit* Illus. by Robert Riger.

> WSP (Archway), 60¢ (5–6)

This is the exciting story of Seabiscuit, a horse who overcomes great odds and makes racing history. Horse lovers especially will appreciate the amount of information on the training and care of horses.

NORTH, STERLING *Rascal*

> Avon (Camelot), 75¢ (6 up)

The story of a young raccoon who was the author's pet in rural Wisconsin when he was 11.

O'DONNELL, JAMES A., McELANEY, PAUL, AND TAYLOR, RAYMOND *Secrets of the Animal World*

> Scholastic (Starline), 50¢ (4–6)

Unusual, humorous, and the peculiar characteristics of many animals are emphasized.

PINNEY, ROY *Pets from the Wood, Field, and Stream,* abridged ed.

> Golden, 75¢ (3–5)

This work includes crows, field mice, turtles, and toads. There is an excellent section on how to build a low cost cage and advice on which pets can be tamed. The author stresses regular care and cleanliness in keeping a pet at home. Includes beautiful color illustrations.

ROUNDS, GLEN *Wild Horses of the Red Desert* Illus. by the author.

> Scholastic, 60¢ (3–5)

Lovely drawings accompany the story of a pack of wild horses, their adventures, and perils through the four seasons in a desert environment.

SELF, MARGARET C. _How and Why Wonder Book of Horses_ Illus. by W. Ferguson.

Wonder, 69¢ (3–5)
If one wants to know about horses in battle, horses of the American West, the hunting and training of horses, and modern horses, this book will help.

SELSAM, MILLICENT _All Kinds of Babies_ Illus. by Symeon Shimin.

Scholastic, 60¢ (K–3)
Young animals and the ways they grow depicted in charming pictures.

SELSAM, MILLICENT _How Animals Sleep_ Illus. by Ezra Jack Keats.

Scholastic, 60¢ (1–3)
The sleeping habits of twenty-four animals and birds as individuals or in groups; of those who sleep by day and those who hibernate. Original title was _A Time for Sleep._

SELSAM, MILLICENT _How Puppies Grow_ Photos by Esther Bubley.

Scholastic, 75¢ (1–3)
Engaging photographs and simple text follow the growth, development, and activities of a litter of puppies from birth to six weeks old.

WOOD, F. DOROTHY _The Mountain Lion and Other Cats_ Photos by Connolly.

Scholastic, 50¢ (3–6)
Black and white action photographs accompany the descriptions of members of the cat family. Among those included are the mountain lion, jaguar, tiger, and house cat. Original title was _The Cat Family._

ZIM, HERBERT S. _The Great Whales_

Scholastic, 50¢ (3–6)
Diverse information about all aspects of the whale and the way he lives is given in a simple fashion. Excellent illustrations are a bonus.

ZIM, HERBERT S., AND HOFFMEISTER, DONALD _Mammals_ Illus. by J. G. Irving.

Golden, $1.25 (3–6)
An informative and instructive guide to North American mam-

mals. Habits and characteristics are accurately described including those of bears, rabbits, deer, and even some extinct mammals.

Biography—Individual and Collective

BAKER, NINA BROWN *Nellie Bly, Reporter*
Scholastic, 60¢ (4–6)
Both girls and boys should enjoy the details of the life of America's first girl reporter and especially of her trip around the world.

BAKER, NINA BROWN *Nickels and Dimes: Story of F. W. Woolworth*
Harcourt (Voyager), 50¢ (6 up)
The inspring account of a poor farm boy's rise to the head of a fabulous merchandising empire.

BAKER, RACHEL *America's First Trained Nurse: Linda Richards*
WSP (Archway), 60¢ (4–6)
Nurse Linda Richards, graduate of America's first nursing school, overcomes primitive and inhumane conditions to bring her patients adequate care. How Linda's ideas and practices brought about a revolution in medical care comprises much of this biography.

BECKHARD, ARTHUR *Albert Einstein*
Avon (Camelot), 50¢ (6 up)
Nobel Prize winner Albert Einstein, the father of atomic physics and man of peace, is portrayed.

BRAYMER, MARJORIE *The Walls of Windy Troy: A Biography of Heinrich Schleimann*
Harcourt (Voyager), 60¢ (6 up)
A competent, well-balanced biography of the 19th century archeologist, Heinrich Schliemann, a man dedicated from childhood to a dream of finding Homer's Troy.

BULLA, CLYDE ROBERT *Squanto, Friend of the Pilgrims* Illus. by Peter Burchard.
Scholastic, 60¢ (3–5)
The true story of an Indian boy who made friends with some early English voyagers to the New World. He journeyed back to England

with them for a visit and returned to America in time to welcome the Pilgrims.

BURLINGAME, ROGER *Inventors Behind the Inventor*
Harcourt (Voyager), 60¢ (6 up)
The accounts of the men behind such geniuses as Morse, Fulton, and Edison. An interestingly contrived presentation that contributes to a better understanding of scientific inventions.

CARRUTH, ELLA KAISER *The Story of Mary McLeod Bethune: She Wanted to Read* Illus. by Herbert McClure
WSP (Archway), 50¢ (4–6)
It was only through determination and stamina that Mary, the fifteenth of seventeen McLeod children, learned to read and write. How this black woman rose from poverty and ignorance to become a world-renowned educator is revealed in this inspiring biography.

CLARK, G. GLENWOOD *Thomas Alva Edison*
Berkley, 50¢ (4–6)
This story of Thomas Alva Edison, scientist and inventor, traces his lifelong quest for scientific knowledge. It is climaxed by his invention of the electric light. Other achievements noted are his invention of the phonograph and motion pictures.

CLAYTON, ED *Martin Luther King: The Peaceful Warrior* Illus. by David Hodges.
WSP (Archway), 60¢ (4–6)
The story of Dr. King's life from childhood in an Atlanta ghetto through high school and college and particularly the events and experiences that molded him for his career as a great leader of non-violence. The latter part of the book emphasizes the major highlights of his career. Numerous illustrations accompany and enhance the text.

COHEN, JOEL H. *Hammerin' Hank of the Braves*
Scholastic, 75¢ (6–8)
This biography of Hank Aaron, one of the all-time greats of baseball, gives an exciting account of his career and has many action photographs.

COLVER, ANNE *Abraham Lincoln* Illus. by William Moyers.
Dell (Yearling), 65¢; Scholastic, 60¢ (2–6)
This easy-to-read biography of Lincoln is told in simple, interesting terms, and is valuable because it is fairly easy to read.

COLVER, ANNE   *Florence Nightingale*   Illus. by Gerald McCann.
Dell (Yearling), 50¢   (2–6)
This is a simple account of the unselfish and courageous nurse, Florence Nightingale.

COMPERE, MICKIE   *The Story of Thomas Alva Edison, Inventor: Wizard of Menlo Park*
Scholastic (Starline), 60¢   (2–3)
An easy-to-read biography of the great inventor.

DAUGHERTY, JAMES   *Abraham Lincoln*
Scholastic, 75¢   (6 up)
This account begins with the early days of the Lincoln family, when Abe's grandparents passed through the Cumberland Gap to the Wilderness Trail in 1809 and his parents were children in the procession. It continues with chapters about Abe—a lawyer in Springfield, his journey to Washington, and his work.

DAVIDSON, MARGARET   *The Adventures of George Washington*
Scholastic, 60¢   (2–3)
A simple biography of our first president, beginning with the French and Indian War.

DAVIDSON, MARGARET   *The Story of Eleanor Roosevelt*
Scholastic, 60¢   (4–6)
A shy, young girl grew to be a brave woman, one of the best-loved in this nation and in others as well.

DOOLEY, THOMAS   *Dr. Tom Dooley, My Story*
NAL (Signet), 75¢   (6–8)
The appealing story of Dr. Tom Dooley's short life is written especially for young people. It is an account of the young doctor's work in Laos and in Vietnam, helping natives in their fight against disease, poverty, and filth.

EATON, JEANETTE   *Lone Journey: The Life of Roger Williams*
Illus. by W. Ishmael.
Harcourt (Voyager), 75¢   (5–7)
A biography of the man who left England to fight for freedom of speech and liberty of worship in colonial America.

FRANK, ANNE   *Diary of a Young Girl*
Pocket, 75¢   (6 up)
Daily reflections of a teenager hiding with her family in a warehouse attic in Holland during the Nazi invasion and occupation.

GRAFF, STEWART, AND GRAFF, P. A. *Helen Keller* Illus. by Paul Frame.

Dell (Yearling), 65¢ (2–4)

An inspiring story of Helen Keller, a blind and deaf girl of great courage.

GRAHAM, SHIRLEY *The Story of Phillis Wheatley: Poetess of the American Revolution* Illus. by R. Brown.

WSP (Archway), 60¢ (6 up)

"But what can a black child *do* with a mind?" Phillis Wheatley, a slave in Boston before the Revolution, wrote poetry, especially on the theme of freedom.

GRAHAM, SHIRLEY, AND LIPSCOMB, GEORGE D. *Dr. George Washington Carver: Scientist*

WSP (Archway), 60¢ (6 up)

An unusually perceptive and well-developed biography of the black man who became one of America's plant scientists.

GRAVES, CHARLES P. *John F. Kennedy* Illus. by Paul Frame.

Dell (Yearling), 65¢ (2–4)

The fascinating life of John F. Kennedy told in terms that can be easily read by young readers.

GREY, ELIZABETH *Friend within the Gates: The Story of Nurse Edith Cavell*

Dell (Yearling), 75¢ (6 up)

The life of the nurse who was executed as a spy during World War I.

HANO, ARNOLD *Willie Mays,* rev. ed.

Grosset (Tempo), 75¢ (6 up)

Biographies of baseball heroes are of interest to both young and older boys. This one, however, reveals much of the personal life as well as the professional life of Willie Mays, and so will be better for older boys.

HATCH, ALDEN *Young Ike* Illus. by Jules Gotlieb.

WSP (Archway), 50¢ (5–8)

This inspiring story of a Kansas farm boy who made it to the presidency of the United States highlights the important events of Dwight Eisenhower's life.

HERRON, EDWARD A. *Wings Over Alaska: The Story of Carl Ben Eielson*
WSP (Archway), 50¢ (4–6)
The first flyer to cross the top of the world and the first to establish airmail service in Alaska.

HICKOK, LORENA *Story of Helen Keller* Illus. by J. Polseno.
Grosset (Tempo), 60¢ (5–7)
A remarkable woman who overcame blindness, deafness, and dumbness to become internationally known.

KILLILEA, MARIE *Wren* Illus. by Robert Riger.
Dell (Yearling), 75¢ (3–7)
Based on the author's bestseller *Karen,* this story is about family life and the loving atmosphere pervading the parents, four children, their many pets, and their Victorian house.

KOMROFF, MANUEL *Marco Polo* Illus. by E. Cirlin.
WSP (Archway), 60¢ (5 up)
This biography is really a rendering of Marco Polo's journals detailing the wonders he encountered on his voyage to Cathay and during his long stay there.

LATHAM, JEAN LEE *Medals for Morse*
Scholastic, 60¢ (4–6)
This biography of Samuel F. B. Morse, told by a Newbery Award winner, provides interesting material on the famous inventor and painter.

LATHAM, JEAN LEE *Sam Houston* Illus. by E. K. Barth and H. Hays.
Dell (Yearling), 50¢ (2–3)
Easy-to-read account of the heroic man who was once governor of Tennessee and later Texas.

LEVINE, I. E. *Young Man in the White House: John Fitzgerald Kennedy*
WSP (Archway), 60¢ (5 up)
This biography of our youngest president contains a very good bibliography and index.

MCGOVERN, ANN *If You Grew Up With Abraham Lincoln* Illus. by Brinton Turkle.
Scholastic, 60¢ (1–3)
This book is full of questions, answers, and stories about Abe

Lincoln. It tells about some of the things one would have seen and done if he had lived in Lincoln's time.

McGOVERN, ANN *Runaway Slave: The Story of Harriet Tubman*
Scholastic, 60¢ (2–4)
An easy-to-read biography of Harriet Tubman, the Moses of her people, who led 300 slaves to freedom.

MALKUS, ALIDA SIMS *Story of Winston Churchill* Illus. by H. B. Vestal.
Grosset (Tempo), 50¢ (4–6)
The remarkable man who led England in its darkest hour during World War II. Will be well received by young people interested in this period of history.

MERRIAM, EVE *The Story of Ben Franklin*
Scholastic, 60¢ (2–3)
An easy-to-read biography of Franklin.

MOORE, EVA *Johnny Appleseed*
Scholastic, 60¢ (1–3)
The legends that have grown up around Johnny Appleseed are added to the historical facts.

PATTERSON, LILLIE *Frederick Douglass: Freedom Fighter* Illus. by Gray Morrow.
Dell (Yearling), 50¢ (4–6)
Born of Southern slave parents, Frederick Douglass broke the bonds of slavery and escaped North. This account of his courage and activities to help free other slaves is complemented by moving full-page illustrations.

ROBINSON, LOUIS, JR. *Arthur Ashe, Tennis Champion*
WSP (Archway), 60¢ (5 up)
This is the inspiring biography of a young black man who, through diligent work, rose to become the first American to win the U. S. Open Championship in tennis. Includes action photographs.

SHAPIRO, MILTON J. *Jackie Robinson of the Brooklyn Dodgers*
WSP(Archway), 60¢ (6 up)
A little baseball, but mostly the story of the problems encountered by the first Negro in major league baseball.

STERLING, DOROTHY *Freedom Train: The Story of Harriet Tubman*
Scholastic, 75¢ (5–7)
Harriet Tubman was an escaped slave who became the symbol of

freedom as time and again she led her people through the underground railroad to freedom.

SULLIVAN, NAVIN *Pioneer Germ Fighters* Illus. by Eric Fraser.
                                    Scholastic, 60¢ (4–6)
Eleven germ fighters including Jenner, Pasteur, Fleming, and Salk.

THORNE, ALICE D. *Story of Madame Curie*
                                    Scholastic, 60¢ (4–6)
The inspiring life of the courageous woman who discovered radium and won a Prize in physics.

WERNSTEIN, IRVING *Man Against the Elements: Adolphus W. Greely*
                                    WSP (Archway), 60¢ (6–9)
The story of a versatile pioneer in Signal Corps strategy, military telegraphy, U. S. Weather Bureau record keeping, and relief work during the San Francisco earthquake.

WOOD, JAMES PLAYSTED AND EDITORS OF *Country Beautiful* MAGAZINE *The Life and Words of John F. Kennedy*
                                    Scholastic, 95¢ (5–6)
Numerous photographs enrich this story of the life of our youngest president. Included are highlights of his school days, military service, courtship of Jacqueline Bouvier, and his political rise to the Senate and Presidency. Excerpts from his speeches add inspirational touches.

History

BAKELESS, KATHERINE, AND BAKELESS, JOHN *Spies of the Revolution*
                                    Scholastic, 60¢ (4–6)
The material in this book is based on *Turncoats, Traitors, and Heroes* by John Bakeless. The emphasis throughout the book is on material that has not been used before. The old spy stories of the Revolution are brought in when they are necessary to the understanding of the history.

BARR, DONALD *How and Why Wonder Book of Primitive Man*
Illus. by M. Kalmenoff.

Wonder, 69¢ (3–5)
Questions about primitive man presented in logical sequence,
followed by factual, scientific answers.

BRANDON, WILLIAM O., ED. *The American Heritage Book of Indians*

Dell (Laurel-Leaf), 75¢ (advanced)
This account is the first to present the history of all Indians
inhabiting North and South America from prehistoric times to the
present. Two maps give tribe locations.

BUCKMASTER, HENRIETTA *Flight to Freedom: The Story of the
Underground Railroad*

Dell (Laurel-Leaf), 50¢ (5–7)
Despite the subtitle, this is the story of the anti-slavery movement
from its earliest efforts through the Reconstruction, with emphasis
on the culpability of the North and on the work of William Lloyd
Garrison. The reader is made to feel "Will we make it? Will we get
slavery abolished?"

CHASE, MARY ELLEN *Sailing the Seven Seas* Illus. by John O'Hara
Cosgrove

Dell (Yearling), 75¢ (4–8)
This true story brings to life the 19th century New England
families who sailed on trim clipper ships and packets to distant
parts—and whose children had the ocean for their home and the
whole world for their school.

COTTRELL, LEONARD *The Horizon Book of Lost Worlds*
Dell (Laurel-Leaf), 75¢ (advanced)
This valuable reference covers nine lost civilizations: Egyptian,
Mycenaean, Mesopotamian, Indus Valley, Minoan, Anatolian,
Etruscan, Khmer, and Mayan.

COTTRELL, LEONARD *Life Under the Pharoahs*
Grosset (Tempo), 75¢ (6 up)
A vivid portrayal of life in Egypt in 1500 B.C. emerges from this
richly detailed and illustrated book.

DOBLER, LAVINIA *Arrow Book of the United Nations*
Scholastic, 60¢ (5 up)
Basic information on the United Nations in question-and-answer
format.

ELTING, MARY, AND FOLSOM, FRANKLIN *If You Lived in the Days of the Wild Mammoth Hunters* Illus. by John Moore.

Scholastic, 60¢ (3–5)

An easy-to-read introduction to archeology and to the customs of man as he roamed the earth in prehistoric times.

GAER, JOSEPH *How the Great Religions Began*

NAL (Signet), 75¢ (advanced)

Emphasis on the foundations and historical backgrounds of the religions rather than their beliefs. Religions covered include: Buddhism, Christianity, Jansenism, Judaism, Mohammedanism, Shinto, Taoism, and Zoroastrianism.

GROSS, RUTH BELOR *Money, Money, Money* Illus. by Leslie Jacobs.

Scholastic, 60¢ (3–4)

Through the ages people have used all sorts of goods for barter and trade. This informative book explains the evolution of trade to the development of monetary systems.

HUREVITZ, HOWARD L. *An Encyclopedic Dictionary of American History*

WSP, $1.45 (5 up)

With a dictionary format, this handy reference book contains concise information on more than 2,500 major American historical events, people, and places.

LANCASTER, BRUCE, AND PLUMB, J. H. *The American Heritage Book of the Revolution*

Dell (Laurel-Leaf), 50¢ (advanced)

A comprehensive history of the Revolution.

LAWSON, ROBERT *Watchwords of Liberty*

Scholastic, 60¢ (5–7)

Provides background behind famous phrases in American history such as "Don't give up the ship" and "What God hath wrought."

McGOVERN, ANN *If You Lived in Colonial Times* Illus. by Brinton Turkle.

Scholastic, 60¢ (2–4)

A simple book that presents information about colonial days in the United States. What people looked like, what happened to the sick, what happened to one who didn't behave in school, and what happened to people who broke the laws are just a few of the situations covered.

McGOVERN, ANN *If You Lived with the Circus* Illus. by Atis Forberg.

Scholastic, 60¢ (3–4)
An inside glimpse into the lives of circus performers. Included are secrets of a clown's make-up, the characteristics of a good animal trainer, and a short section on circus lingo.

McGOVERN, ANN *If You Sailed on the Mayflower* Illus. by J. B. Handelsman.

Scholastic, 60¢ (K–3)
Entertaining and informative, this little book answers many questions about the first Pilgrims to reach America—how they lived on the ship, what happened when they landed on shore, and the like. Included is a cutaway drawing of the Mayflower.

MAGINLEY, C. J. *Historic Models of Early America and How to Make Them* Illus. by J. MacDonald.

Harcourt (Voyager), 60¢ (6 up)
Clear pictures, a list of material needed, and instructions for making models of objects used in early America, including a cabin and a ducking stool.

MIERS, EARL S. *America and Its Presidents*

Grosset (Tempo), 75¢ (6 up)
Useful, illustrated material of the presidents of the United States.

MILLER, JOHN C. *The First Frontier: Life in Colonial America,* abridged ed.

Dell (Laurel-Leaf), 75¢ (6 up)
Portrays the everyday experiences of the colonists as told through letters, diaries, comments of travelers, and public documents.

MOODY, RALPH *Riders of the Pony Express* Illus. by R. Riger.

Dell (Yearling), 75¢ (6 up)
A detailed account of the first Pony Express ride, highlights of later trips, and cursory biographical information of the most famous riders.

MONTROSS, LYNN, AND MILLER, WILLIAM *The United States Marines*

Dell (Yearling), 75¢ (6 up)
The U. S. Marines, from the Corps' founding to Korea.

PARKMAN, FRANCIS *The Oregon Trail*

Airmont, 50¢; Bantam, 50¢ (6 up)
A fascinating and true record of the adventures of Parkman and

four companions when they joined the great westward movement in 1846.

Spencer, Philip *Day of Glory: The Guns at Lexington and Concord* Illus. by Peter Burchard.

Scholastic, 75¢ (4–6)

The events of every hour on April 19, 1775, march through the pages in this exciting account of the start of the American Revolution.

Zim, Herbert, and Florida Museum Staff *American Southeast* Illus. by B. and S. Barlowe.

Golden, $1.95 (3–5)

Basic reference material for the Southeastern United States is presented. It gives the reader a quick grasp of much information about this part of the country.

Language

Epstein, Sam, and Epstein, Beryl *What's Behind the Word?* Illus. by George Wilde.

Scholastic, 60¢ (5–8)

Here is the story of words—their histories and mysteries. The meanings of names, the origins of surnames, and the secrets and origins of words are explained. Adapted from *The First Book of Words.*

Guralnik, D. B., ed. *Webster's New World Dictionary of the American Language*

Popular, 75¢ (4 up)

A basic dictionary with examples to clarify definitions.

Lewis, Norman, ed. *The New Roget's Thesaurus in Dictionary Form*

Berkley (Medallion), 75¢ (6 up)

This guide contains an alphabetical listing of words with their synonyms, antonyms, and cross-references. Included are slang words, colloquialisms, and scientific terms.

New Merriam Webster Pocket Dictionary With a New 1970 Supplement
> Pocket (Cardinal ed.), 75¢ (5 up)

Added informative features include: population figures for the U. S. and Canada, a 1970 supplement of new words, foreign words and phrases, and abbreviations.

Scholastic Dictionary of American English   Illus. by Alan Young.
> Scholastic, $1.65 (4–8)

A special helpful section teaches the child how to use the dictionary—finding words, keys to pronunciation, and the like. Following the word listings are tables with vital historical information on North America.

Scholastic Dictionary of Synonyms, Antonyms, and Homonyms
> Scholastic, 75¢ (4 up)

This handy collection of more than 20,000 synonyms and antonyms will help the student (and adult) to expand his vocabulary and express himself more effectively. Words are listed in alphabetical order.

Leisure Activities—Games, Hobbies, and Sports

ARNOLD, WESLEY F., AND CARDY, WAYNE C.   *Fun with Next to Nothing*   Illus. by the authors.
> Scholastic, 60¢ (3–5)

Simple instructions for making things from easy-to-obtain materials make this book an invaluable aid for parents and teachers as well as fun for children. Items are grouped into units such as transportation, shelter, space ships, and so on.

BALET, JAN   *What Makes an Orchestra,* abridged ed.
> Scholastic, 60¢ (3–7)

A picture of one of the instruments that make up an orchestra appears on each page.

CARLSON, BERNICE W.   *Act It Out*
> Abingdon, $1.60 (4–6)

The first section contains different types of plays, pantomimes,

stunts, and tableaux for the reader to perform. The second part
tells how to make various puppets and provides plays for them to
perform in.

CARLSON, BERNICE W. *Do it Yourself: Tricks, Stunts and Skits*
Illus. by Laszlo Matulay.

Abingdon, $1.60 (4–7)
The subtitle says it all.

CARLSON, BERNICE W. *Make it and Use it* Illus. by Aline Hansens.
Abingdon, $1.60
Make it out of plain paper, crepe paper, newspaper, cardboard,
boxes, food, cloth, or anything else you can find.

CARLSON, BERNICE W. *Right Play for You* Illus. by G. Boris.
Abingdon, $1.60 (5 up)
The production of a play with emphasis on developing your own
ideas and examples to illustrate the different types of plays that
can be put on.

CHERNOFF, GOLDIE TAUB *Just a Box?* Illus. by Margaret Hartelius.
Scholastic, 75¢ (2–4)
Simple instructions and diagrams for making creative toys and
useful items out of empty household boxes (cereal, tissue, etc.) are
easy enough for a child to understand and also provide many
helpful hints for parents and teachers.

DALE, RALPH ALAN *Games to Sing and Play* Illus. by Olivia H. H.
Cole.

Scholastic, 60¢ (1–3)
A selection of familiar fun-to-play singing games has accompanying illustrations and directions. Among the favorites are "Skip-
to-My-Lou" and "In-and-Out-the-Window."

GOLDSMITH, LYNNE, (ADAPTER) *A Christmas Carol*
Scholastic, 50¢ (3–4)
A literary classic adapted as a play is especially suited to school
use. A list of props and costumes and two familiar Christmas
carols are included.

HARBIN, ELVIN O. *Games for Boys and Girls* Illus. by K. J. Murr.
Abingdon, $1.65 (3–7)
Clear directions and detailed pictures for playing 262 indoor and
outdoor games, noisy games and quiet games, games for small
groups and games for crowds. An old favorite even better in
paperback.

JACKSON, C. PAUL *How to Play Better Baseball* Illus. by Leonard Kessler.

> Scholastic, 75¢ (5–8)
> This guide is packed with information on baseball terms, equipment, and playing techniques. Drawings help clarify important points.

KETTELKAMP, LARRY *Magic Made Easy*

> Scholastic, 60¢ (4–7)
> The author stresses optical illusions for his first simple tricks. Then, using props found in any home, he does easy magic tricks, progressing to more difficult ones.

KETTELKAMP, LARRY *Spooky Magic*

> Scholastic, 60¢ (4–7)
> This follow-up to *Magic Made Easy* includes twelve tricks for the young magician to conjure with. The directions are clear and detailed with adequate preparation and patience emphasized.

KLEIN, LEONORE *Arrow Book of Tricks and Projects* Illus. by William Meyerriecks.

> Scholastic, 50¢ (3–5)
> For the child interested in tricks and projects: includes secret talk, doodling with numbers, making a puppet, eye foolers, and science tricks.

MACFARLAN, ALLAN *The Boy's Book of Biking* Illus. by Paulette Macfarlan.

> WSP (Archway), 60¢ (4–8)
> This comprehensive guide provides valuable information on buying a bicycle, accessories, care of bikes, trip tips, and the like. All children who are interested in bicycling will benefit from reading this book.

MASIN, HERMAN L. *How to Star in Baseball.*

> Scholastic, 60¢ (4–6)
> Clearly divided into sections—pitching, base running, playing the infield, and so on. Well-illustrated with many pages of photographs and playing tips.

MERVIS, RABBI LEONARD J. *We Celebrate the Jewish Holidays*

> Union, $1.50 (5 up)
> This is a concise collection of Jewish customs, songs, games, and foods incorporated into Jewish holidays and celebrations. Included are illustrated instructions for making charming decorations.

MILLEN, NINA *Children's Festivals from Many Lands* Illus. by Janet Smalley.

> Friendship, $2.95 (4–6)

Celebrations, holy days, and folk festivals of many lands are described in this enjoyable, informative book. Included are greetings from various countries.

MILLEN, NINA *Children's Games from Many Lands,* revised ed. Illus. by Allan Eitzen.

> Friendship, $2.95 (4–6)

This lively collection of games and songs from many countries will bring hours of enjoyment and fun to young children. Helpful ideas for teachers and parents.

PERKINS, WILMA L. *Fannie Farmer Junior Cook Book,* rev. ed. Illus. by M. P. Getchell.

> Bantam, 75¢ (4–6)

Based on the sound teaching rules and the clear, standard recipes of the famous *Boston Cooking-School Cook Book.*

ROCKOWITZ, MURRAY *Arrow Book of Word Games* Illus. by William Hogarth.

> Scholastic, 50¢ (4–6)

Word games, brain teasers, and crossword puzzles made interesting by the illustrations and easy-to-read type.

RYP, ELLEN STERN, ED. *Arrow Book of Baseball Fun* Illus. by George Wilder.

> Scholastic, 60¢ (5–6)

Puzzles, quizzes, capsule stories of famous players, interesting statistics, and more are packed into this book for the young baseball fan.

WEISS, HARVEY *Pencil, Pen and Brush*

> Scholastic, 75¢ (4–6)

This is truly a how-to-draw book. The author gives explicit and concise directions on how to draw animals, figures, and heads from imagination and still life. The directions give information on materials as well. Includes useful illustrations and pictures.

ZIM, HERBERT S. *Codes and Secret Writing,* abridged ed.

> Scholastic, 60¢ (5 up)

With his usual clarity, Mr. Zim teaches the reader how to communicate with friends by using simple codes. There are two entire chapters on secret writing and invisible inks. The book includes answers to the exercises.

Natural History

AMES, GERALD, AND WYLER, ROSE *First Days of the World* Illus. by Leonard Weisgard.

Scholastic, 60¢ (3–5)

The formation of the earth, the beginnings of life, and the evolution of plants and prehistoric animals are described.

BARKER, WILL *Fresh Water Friends and Foes*

Acropolis, $1.95 (4–8)

Primarily a guide to various fresh water environments and their inhabitants, this book also emphasizes how man is destroying his rivers, lakes, and ponds. Numerous pictures illustrate the text.

BOYLE, E. MARIE *Seedless Plants: Soil Builders*

Beacon, 75¢ (4–6)

The story of how flora such as mosses, ferns, and lichen rebuild the soil.

BUCK, MARGARET WARING *Along the Seashore* Illus. by the author.

Abingdon, $1.75 (4–6)

Detailed drawings describe many kinds of plant and animal life surrounding the continental United States.

BUCK, MARGARET WARING *In Ponds and Streams* Illus. by the author.

Abingdon, $1.75 (4–6)

Insects, plants, and animals found in and around ponds and streams. Simple drawings of life cycles and of basic means of identification.

BUCK, MARGARET WARING *In Woods and Fields* Illus. by the author.

Abingdon, $1.75 (4–6)

A guide, arranged by season, to birds, insects, and flowers commonly found in North America.

CLYMER, ELEANOR *Search for a Living Fossil*

Scholastic (Starline), 60¢ (3–5)

The first coelacanth was lost to science for lack of refrigeration. It was 14 years before the South African scientist located another, and he lost that one too for lack of refrigeration, communication, transportation, and governmental support.

Coe, Geoffrey, and Sutton, Felix *How and Why Wonder Book of Fish*
Wonder, 69¢ (3–5)
Factual answers to questions on the subject of fish.

Cooper, Elizabeth K. *Science in Your Own Back Yard*
Harcourt (Voyager), 65¢ (4–6)
Exploring one's own yard by lying on your stomach and on your back lets one investigate soil, grass, flowers, small animals, birds, clouds, weather, and stars.

Cooper, Elizabeth K. *Science on the Shores and Banks*
Harcourt (Voyager), 60¢ (4–6)
A science hobby book in which the author invites the young reader to experiment following the scientific method. Many forms of small insect and animal creatures and plants that live at the edge of the water, on bank or shore, and in tide pools are described.

Craig, M. Jean *Questions and Answers About Weather* Illus. by Maija Kaljo.
Scholastic, 60¢ (4–6)
A book of questions and answers frequently asked by boys and girls about the weather. Very simple, but abstract-type paintings in color are delightful.

Duvall, Evelyn Mills *About Sex and Growing Up* Illus. by Simon Frankel.
Association, $1.50 (5–)
This informative, straight-forward book combines pertinent information on sex with emotional and social problems of pre-teen years. Helpful vocabulary lists appear after each chapter.

Hoss, Norman James *How and Why Wonder Book of Stars* Illus. by J. Ponter.
Wonder, 69¢ (3–5)
Thoughtful questions, which are printed in boldface type, that might occur to the student as he begins to explore the subject of the stars.

Hyler, Nelson W. *How and Why Wonder Book of Rocks and Minerals* Illus. by K. Shannon.
Wonder, 69¢ (3–5)
Questions about rocks and minerals are answered in a logical and scientific manner.

IRVING, ROBERT *Hurricanes and Twisters*
Scholastic, 60¢ (4–6)
The causes, nature, and disastrous results of hurricanes and tornados are vividly described.

KEEN, MARTIN L. *How and Why Wonder Book of the Human Body* Illus. by D. Sweet.
Wonder, 69¢ (3–5)
Information about the human body in question-and-answer form.

LAUBER, PATRICIA *Junior Science Book of Icebergs and Glaciers*
Scholastic, 60¢ (4–6)
Elementary introduction to icebergs, glaciers, and ice ages.

LINDSAY, BARBARA *Monsters of the Sea* Illus. by William Bartlett.
Scholastic, 50¢ (3–6)
This text is filled with drawings, photos, and descriptions of some of the strangest of ocean-dwelling creatures. Included in the book are jellyfish, stingrays, giant 500-pound clams, plus many others.

LOW, DONALD F. *How and Why Wonder Book of Sea Shells* Illus. by C. and A. Koehler.
Wonder, 69¢ (3–5)
Questions about many of the common sea shells elicit information on the animals who lived in them.

MAY, JULIAN *They Turned to Stone* Illus. by Jean Zallinger.
Scholastic, 60¢ (1–2)
This is a simple, factual account of how ferns, animals, and fish were preserved in stone and became fossils.

PRINGLE, LAURENCE *The Only Earth We Have*
Macmillan (Collier), $1.60 (5–8)
The scope of pollution (air, water, pesticides, etc.) is covered in this informative book with accompanying photographs. Included are the names and addresses of conservation groups.

REY, H. A. *Know the Stars* Illus. by the author.
Scholastic, 75¢ (3–6)
The format is very much the same as *Find the Constellations,* from which it was abridged, with the essential material included. The child can use this book to find all the constellations in the sky.

Rood, Ronald N. *How and Why Wonder Book of Ants and Bees*
Illus. by C. and A. Koehler.

Wonder, 69¢ (3–5)
Considerable information is given in answer to questions about
bees, wasps, ants, and termites.

Rood, Ronald N. *How and Why Wonder Book of Insects*
Wonder, 69¢ (3–5)
Questions on insects presented in logical sequence, followed by
factual answers.

Schneider, Leo *You and Your Senses* Illus. by G. Schrotter.
Harcourt (Voyager), 50¢ (4–6)
A scientific explanation of how the five outer senses report on the
everyday world. It also explores the important inner senses, such
as hunger and thirst, and includes a fascinating chapter on the
brain.

Selsam, Millicent *The Birth of an Island* Illus. by Winifred
Lubell.

Scholastic, 50¢ (3–5)
An account of how a tropical volcanic island developed a plant
cover and eventually supported 573 species of animals.

Selsam, Millicent *Questions and Answers About Ants* Illus. by
Arabelle Wheatley.

Scholastic, 60¢ (1–3)
An introduction to ants, including the care of a colony.

Shapp, Martha, and Shapp, Charles *Let's Find Out About the
Moon*

Scholastic, 50¢ (K–3)
Information about the moon for the very youngest, including what
the astronauts are likely to discover.

Stefferud, Alfred *The Wonders of Seeds* Illus. by S. Briggs.
Harcourt (Voyager), 45¢ (4–6)
This fascinating story tells how seeds sprout, grow, flower, and
bear fruit filled with new seeds. There are simple experiments for
young botanists.

Sterling, Dorothy *The Story of Caves*
Scholastic, 60¢ (5 up)
Explanations of how the various types of caves and caverns are
formed. Miscellaneous facts about famous ones, and information
on cave pictures, exploring, and related subjects are included.

SUTTON, FELIX   *How and Why Wonder Book of Our Earth*
Wonder, 69¢ (3–5)
Questions about the earth presented in a logical sequence, followed by factual answers.

SUTTON, FELIX   *How and Why Wonder Book of Deserts*   Illus. by R. Doremus.
Wonder, 69¢ (3–5)
Questions about the desert presented in a logical sequence, followed by informative answers.

ZIM, HERBERT S.   *Alligators and Crocodiles.*
Scholastic, 60¢ (4–6)
Valuable information includes how these animals breathe and swim, where they live, the laying and hatching of their eggs, and what they eat and how they get it.

ZIM, HERBERT S.   *Snakes*   Illus. by J. G. Irving.
Scholastic, 60¢ (4–7)
The life habits of snakes, the identification of poisonous snakes, and an explanation of some of the myths about snakes. Unfortunately, the illustrations are in black and white.

ZIM, HERBERT S., AND BAKER, R. H.   *Stars*   Illus. by J. G. Irving.
Golden, $1.25 (4–6)
An authoritative, carefully organized book for quick reference on stars.

ZIM, HERBERT S. AND COTTAM, C. A.   *Insects*   Illus. by J. G. Irving.
Golden, $1.25 (3–6)
An authentic pocket-size manual on insects, their growth stages, and other pertinent data for the young naturalist. This will be useful to both students and teachers.

ZIM, HERBERT S., AND GABRIELSON, IRA   *Birds*   Illus. by J. G. Irving.
Golden, $1.25 (4–7)
Authoritative basic data for identifying related species. Gives information on where and how to look for birds.

ZIM, HERBERT S., AND INGLE, LESTER   *Seashores*   Illus. by D. and S. Barlowe.
Golden, $1.25 (3–6)
An authoritative pocket guide to animals and plants found along the beaches. Useful for identification purposes.

ZIM, HERBERT S., AND MARTIN, A. C. *Flowers* Illus. by R. Freund.
Golden, $1.25 (4–7)
A Golden Nature Guide that is a practical beginner's guide for
study and identification of flowers, characteristics of flowers, and
their habitats. Family and growing seasons are given.

ZIM, HERBERT S., AND MARTIN, A. C. *Trees* Illus. by D. and S.
Barlowe.
Golden, $1.25 (4–6)
Informative material on familiar American trees, pointing out
features important in identification.

ZIM, HERBERT S., AND SHAFFER, PAUL R. *Rocks and Minerals*
Illus. by R. Perlman.
Golden, $1.25 (3–6)
An informative guide for studying familiar rocks and minerals;
also useful for identification and classification.

ZIM, HERBERT S., AND SHOEMAKER, HURST *Fishes* Illus. by J. G.
Irving.
Golden, $1.25 (4–7)
Authoritative basic information provides a guide to fresh- and
salt-water fish. It tells how fish may best be studied, identified, and
classified.

ZIM, HERBERT S. AND SMITH, HOBART M. *Reptiles and Amphibians*
Illus. by J. G. Irving.
Golden, $1.25 (3–6)
A guide to the familiar American species, with authoritative
descriptions of the species and how to study them.

Science

BARROW, GEORGE *Your World in Motion: The Story of Energy*
Illus. by M. Waltrip.
Harcourt (Voyager), 60¢ (5 up)
Motion in water, air, light, and electricity, the energy these
motions produce, and the use man makes of it.

BULLA, CLYDE ROBERT   *What Makes a Shadow?*   Illus. by Adriene Adams.
                                  Scholastic (Starline), 75¢   (3–5)
A colorful picture book showing how shadows are made by different objects, how their size and intensity may be changed, and how shadow pictures may be projected onto a wall.

FREEMAN, MAE   *A Book of Real Science*
                                  Scholastic (Starline), 50¢   (K–2)
Elementary introduction to molecules, electricity, heat, light, sound, and gravity.

FREEMAN, MAE   *The Real Magnet Book*
                                  Scholastic (Starline), 60¢   (K–3)
What makes a magnet a magnet, what it does, and some things to do with it.

FREEMAN, MAE   *The Wonderful Looking-Through Glass*
                                  Scholastic, 75¢   (3–5)
Some of the many wonders revealed by a magnifying glass are discussed in this book of experiments. A small magnifying glass is included so the child can explore for himself.

KEEN, MARTIN L.   *How and Why Wonder Book of Chemistry*   Illus. by W. Furguson.
                                  Wonder, 69¢   (3–5)
Questions about chemistry are answered in a logical and scientific manner.

KEEN, MARTIN L.   *How and Why Wonder Book of Science Experiments*   Illus. by G. Zaffo.
                                  Wonder, 69¢   (3–5)
The text provides answers to many questions about science.

KNIGHT, CLAYTON   *How and Why Wonder Book of Rockets and Missiles*
                                  Wonder, 69¢   (3–5)
Questions on rockets and missiles presented in logical sequence.

MILGRAM, HARRY   *Explorations in Science: A Book of Basic Experiments*   Illus. by Ann Marie Jauss.
                                  Dutton, $1.25   (5–6)
Many simple and interesting experiments explain basic scientific principles. Most equipment for the experiments is easily obtainable.

MORGAN, ALFRED *First Chemistry Book for Boys and Girls* Illus. by B. Babbitt and T. Smith.

Scribner, $1.65 (4–6)

Many interesting experiments—simple safe, and simple to carry out—are illustrated for easy execution.

NOTKIN, JEROME J., AND GULKIN, S. *How and Why Wonder Book of Electricity* Illus. by R. Patterson and C. Bernard.

Wonder, 69¢ (3–5)

Many factual answers are given on the subject of electricity.

PINE, TILLIE S. *The Indians Knew,* abridged ed. Illus. by Ezra Jack Keats.

Scholastic, 60¢ (2–3)

The Indians made use of many scientific principles that we also use today. Simple experiments to illustrate them are given.

PINE, TILLIE S., AND LEVINE, JOSEPH *Magnets and How to Use Them* Illus. by Bernice Myers.

Scholastic, 75¢ (2–3)

An enjoyable book for the young child to use in experimenting with magnets. The reader can find out what to do with a magnet by using the one enclosed in the book.

SCHNEIDER, HERMAN, AND SCHNEIDER, NINA *How Big Is Big?* Illus. by Symeon Shimin.

Scholastic, 60¢ (2–4)

A discussion of size, starting with the elephant and progressing to the largest stars; then starting with the reader and going down to atoms.

SCHNEIDER, NINA, AND SCHNEIDER, HERMAN *Let's Find Out About Heat, Weather, and Air* Illus. by Jeanne Bendick.

Scholastic, 60¢ (2–4)

Simple experiments demonstrating the effects of heat and the uses made of air.

WYLER, ROSE *Real Science Riddles* Illus. by Talivaldis Stubis.

Scholastic, 50¢ (2–4)

Many interesting riddles with scientific answers are included. Some simple experiments are explained.

WYLER, ROSE, AND AMES, GERALD *Prove It!* Illus. by Talivaldis Stubis

Scholastic, 60¢ (1–3)

Simple science experiments using things found around the house.

MYTHS, FOLKLORE, AND FAIRY TALES

The Adventures of Spider: West African Folk Tales Retold by Joyce Cooper Arkhurst.   Illus. by Jerry Pinkney.
                                    Scholastic, 75¢   (3–5)
   A collection of six tales about Spider who hails from the jungles of West Africa. He is clever, mischievous, and finds himself in many unpredictable situations.

AESOP   *City Mouse-Country Mouse* (and two more tales from Aesop) Illus. by Marian Parry.
                                    Scholastic, 75¢   (K–2)
   Three imaginatively illustrated mouse tales by Aesop have important morals as well as bringing entertainment to the reader.

Aesop's Fables   Ed. by Joseph Jacobs.   Illus. by David Levine.
                                    Schocken, $1.75   (K–up)
   A collection of beast tales that illustrate morals or precepts.

ANDERSEN, HANS CHRISTIAN   *Andersen's Fairy Tales,* ed. by Freya Littledale.
                                    Scholastic, 60¢   (4–6)
   This collection includes nine classic tales such as "Thumbelina" and "The Princess and the Pea." It will be useful on occasions when Andersen's stories are appropriate.

ANDERSEN, HANS CHRISTIAN   *The Emperor's New Clothes* Illus. by Virginia Lee Burton.
                                    Scholastic, 75¢   (K–4)
   This is as close as Andersen gets to humor. It takes a child to pierce

the pretensions of the adults who are afraid to admit their deficiencies.

ANDERSEN, HANS CHRISTIAN *Snow Queen and Other Tales* Illus. by Greenwald.

NAL (Signet), 75¢ (4–6)

This book contains forty-seven of the world's most loved fairy tales.

CONGER, LESLEY *Three Giant Stories* Illus. by Rosalind Fry.

Scholastic, 60¢ (2–4)

Three stories are retold here: "The Giant and the Cobbler," based on an account in *The Minor Traditions of British Mythology* by Lewis Spence; "The Brave Little Tailor," from the versions found in many countries; and "How Big-Mouth Wrestled the Giant," based on various folklore motifs.

COOLIDGE, OLIVIA, ED. *Hercules and Other Tales from Greek Myths,* abridged ed. Illus. by David Lockhart.

Scholastic (Starline), 60¢ (4–6)

Some of the more familiar of the Greek myths told as complete stories. Original title was *Greek Myths.*

GREEN, ROGER L., ED. *Tale of Troy*

Penguin (Puffin), $1.45 (6–9)

A retelling of the Trojan War.

GREEN, ROGER L., ED. *Tales of the Greek Heroes*

Penguin (Puffin), 95¢ (6–9)

A selection of myths telling the deeds of the famous heroes.

GREEN, ROGER L., ED. *Robin Hood*

Penguin (Puffin), 95¢ (5 up)

The stories of Robin Hood and his adventures with the king's foresters in Sherwood Forest. An excellent edition.

GRIMM BROTHERS *Household Stories from the Collection of the Brothers Grimm*

Dover, $2.00 (4–6)

A collection of folk tales gathered by the Grimm Brothers mainly from 1812 to 1815.

HAMILTON, EDITH *Mythology*

NAL (Mentor), 95¢ (6–9)

A comprehensive compilation of Greek and Roman myths, with some Norse ones included.

JACOBS, JOSEPH, ED. *Celtic Fairy Tales* Illus. by J. D. Batten.
Dover, $1.75 (4–6)
This volume of twenty-six Celtic folk tales introduces children to
the special vision, color, and unique imagination of the Celts.
More Celtic Fairy Tales is also available from Dover for $1.75.

JACOBS, JOSEPH, ED. *English Fairy Tales* Illus. by J. D. Batten.
Dover, $1.75; Schocken, $1.95 (4–6)
An outstanding collection of fairy tales from the folklore of the
British Isles. Rewritten by Joseph Jacobs to preserve their humor
and dramatic power and to simplify the dialect.

KEDABRA, ABBY, ED. *Nine Witch Tales* Illus. by John Fernie.
Scholastic, 60¢ (4–6)
A collection of nine spine-tingling tales of witches and sorceresses
from many lands, including "The Hungry Old Witch" and "The
Cat Witch." Very attractive format adds flavor.

LANG, ANDREW, ED. *Blue Fairy Book* Illus. by H. J. Ford and G.
Hood.
Dover, $1.95 (4–6)
Composed almost entirely of the "older" favorite fairy tales—"Cin-
derella," "Jack the Giant Killer," "Snow White and Rose Red," and
"Why the Sea Is Salt"—this will be valuable to teachers as fine
material for reading in the literature program.

LANG, ANDREW, ED. *Brown Fairy Book* Illus. by H. J. Ford.
Dover, $2.00 (4–6)
A beautiful edition of fairy tales gathered from many countries
and sources. Useful to the teacher reading to her class.

LANG, ANDREW, ED. *Crimson Fairy Book* Illus. by H. J. Ford.
Dover, $2.50 (4–6)
Fairy tales gathered from many sources and countries; another of
the beautiful editions giving additional tales.

LANG, ANDREW, ED. *Pink Fairy Book* Illus. by H. J. Ford.
Dover, $2.00 (4–6)
This collection contains 41 from Japan, Italy, Africa, and Scandi-
navia.

LANG, ANDREW, ED. *Red Fairy Book* Illus. by H. J. Ford and L.
Speed.
Dover, $2.00 (4–6)
This was the second of Lang's collections, including many old
favorites such as "Jack and the Beanstalk" and "Rapunzel."

Lang, Andrew, ed. *The Story of Robin Hood and Other Tales of Adventure and Battle* Illus. by H. J. Ford.
Schocken, $1.75 (5 up)
The stories of Robin Hood and his adventures with the king's foresters in Sherwood Forest make exciting reading. This band of outlaws robbed the rich and helped the poor during the reign of Henry II of England.

Lang, Andrew, ed. *Tales from the Green Fairy Book,* abridged ed. Illus. by Hertha Depper.
Scholastic (Starline), 60¢ (4–6)
Eleven fairy tales such as "The Ugly Shepherdess" and "Little One-Eye, Little Two-Eyes and Little Three-Eyes."

Lang, Andrew, ed. *Tales from the Red Fairy Book,* abridged ed. Illus. by Irma Wilde.
Scholastic (Starline), 60¢ (4–6)
Eight fairy tales, including such favorites as "The Twelve Dancing Princesses" and "The Golden Goose."

Lang, Andrew, ed. *Violet Fairy Book* Illus. by H. J. Ford and H. J. Lang.
Dover, $2.50 (4–6)
Includes "Tale of the Tontawald," "Finest Liar in the World," and "Three Wonderful Beggars." Another beautiful edition.

Lang, Andrew, ed. *Yellow Fairy Book* Illus. by H. J. Ford.
Dover, $2.00 (4–6)
Another fine Dover edition, which contains such stories as "Cat and the Mouse," "Six Swans," and "Dragon the North."

McCormick, Dell J. *Paul Bunyan Swings His Axe* Illus. by Leo Summers.
Scholastic, 50¢ (3–5)
Humorous tales about the giant woodsman and his blue ox. Illustrations add color to the text of this favorite yarn.

Ozaki, Yei T., ed. *Japanese Fairy Book* Illus. by K. Fujiyama.
Dover, $1.95 (4–6)
Contains a delightful collection of twenty-two popular Japanese fairy tales. Delightful reading for the young and old alike.

Pyle, Howard *Pepper and Salt, or Seasoning for Young People*
Dover, $2.00 (4–6)
Fairy tales reminiscent of Grimms' with delightful poems and many painless morals.

PYLE, HOWARD *Story of King Arthur and His Knights*
Dover, $2.50 (4–6)
The favorite legends of King Arthur and his Knights of the Round Table told with the style and imagination characteristic of this famous author.

PYLE, HOWARD, AND PYLE, KATHERINE *The Wonder Clock*
Dover, $3.00 (4–7)
Twenty-four marvelous tales—one for each hour of the day—in this companion volume to *Pepper and Salt*. Included are such stories as "Bearskin," "Water of Life," and "Master Jacob."

The Teeny Tiny Woman: A Folktale Illus. by Margot Zemach.
Scholastic, 50¢ (1–3)
The size of the book matches the size of the heroine in this favorite English folktale. Well illustrated.

Tikki Tikki Tembo Retold by Arlene Mosel. Illus. by Blair Lent.
Scholastic, 75¢ (3–5)
This delightful Chinese tale of the adventures of two small brothers tells us why we should give children short names. Lovely illustrations add interest to the story.

UCHIDA, YOSHIKO *The Magic Listening Cap: More Folk Tales from Japan*
Harcourt (Voyager), 75¢ (3–5)
Fourteen Japanese folk tales with universal themes that will appeal to children everywhere.

WILDE, OSCAR *Happy Prince and Other Stories*
Penguin (Puffin), 95¢ (3–6)
Wilde's own delightful fairy tales made up for reading aloud to his own children.

POETRY, RHYMES, RIDDLES, AND JOKES

ADOFF, ARNOLD, ED. *I Am the Darker Brother: An Anthology of Modern Poems by Black Americans* Illus. by Benny Andrews.
Macmillan (Collier), $1.25 (6 up)
This collection of moving, eloquent poems brings into sharp focus the harsh realities, emotions, and thoughts that are so much with the black man today.

ALDIS, DOROTHY *The Secret Place and Other Poems* Illus. by Olivia H. H. Cole.
Scholastic, 50¢ (2–4)
Poetry for children about familiar things. The illustrations enhance the beauty of the book.

COLE, WILLIAM, ED. *Oh, What Nonsense* Illus. by Tomi Ungerer.
Viking (Seafarer), 65¢ (4–6)
This witty collection of poems, well suited to any child, is coupled with adorable poker-faced characters to make for very light-hearted reading.

CRAMPTON, GERTRUDE *Your Own Joke Book*
Scholastic (Starline), 50¢ (2–6)
Limericks and funny stories that will appeal to all elementary students.

Funny Jokes and Foxy Riddles Illus. by Allan Jaffee.
Golden, 75¢ (all ages)
The book has such riddles as "What did Paul Revere say at the end of his ride?" ("Whoa"), and new ones as well.

GRAHAM, ELEANOR, ED.   *Puffin Book of Verse*
Penguin (Puffin), 95¢
A child will treasure a copy of this for his very own. Here are nursery rhymes, nonsense poems, and serious works of interest to a child. A colorful cover and excellent paper complete the beauty of the book.

HOPKINS, LEE BENNETT, AND ARENSTEIN, MISHA, EDS.   *Faces and Places: Poems for You*   Illus. by Lisl Weil.
Scholastic, 60¢   (3–6)
This enjoyable book of poems is geared to tickle youngsters' fancies. Illustrations are simple but quite charming.

ISSA, YAYU, AND OTHER JAPANESE POETS   *Don't Tell the Scarecrow and Other Japanese Poems*   Illus. by Talivaldis Stubis.
Scholastic, 75¢   (K–2)
A charming edition of Oriental poetry. Thirty-four short poems, mainly by well-known poets.

LEAR, EDWARD   *Complete Nonsense*
Dover, $2.00   (2 up)
Verse, prose, drawings, alphabets, and other funny things to tickle the young reader. A book for all ages that will be useful whenever the situation calls for nonsense verse and especially that of Edward Lear.

LEAR, EDWARD   *Nonsense Books of Edward Lear*
NAL (Signet), 75¢   (2 up)
All the rhymes and nonsense selections of Edward Lear.

McGOVERN, ANN, ED.   *Arrow Book of Poetry*   Illus. by Grisha Dotzenko.
Scholastic, 60¢   (4–6)
A collection of children's poetry with intriguing illustrations in soft varied shades of green that capture the interest of the reader.

MORRISON, LILLIAN, ED.   *Remember Me When This You See,* abridged ed.   Illus. by Marjorie Bauernschmidt.
Scholastic, 60¢   (6 up)
Lively collection of chuckle-provoking autograph-book verses and sayings.

MORRISON, LILLIAN, ED.   *Yours Till Niagara Falls,* abridged ed. Illus. by Marjorie Bauernschmidt.
Scholastic, 50¢   (4 up)
Contains the best verses and sayings that the young write in autograph books.

Opie, Iona, and Opie, Peter   *Puffin Book of Nursery Rhymes*
                    Penguin (Puffin), $1.25   (K–2)
A fine edition containing a sparkling treasury of memorable
verses. Indexed by subject and first lines.

Sandburg, Carl   *Wind Song*   Illus. by W. A. Smith.
                    Harcourt (Voyager), 45¢   (2–5)
A collection of poems selected by Carl Sandburg for the young.

Stevenson, Robert L.   *Child's Garden of Verses*
        Airmont, 50¢; Penguin (Puffin), 95¢; Pyramid, 35¢   (K–4)
A collection of cherished poems.

Winn, Marie, and Ott, Phyllis   *Riddles, Rhymes, and Jokes #1*
Illus. by Stan Robinson.
                    Young Readers, 60¢   (3–6)
This little book is chock full of zany rhymes, jokes, riddles,
crossword puzzles, and challenging and interesting games.

Winn, Marie, and Ott, Phyllis   *Riddles, Rhymes, and Jokes
#2*   Illus. by Stan Robinson.
                    Young Readers, 60¢   (3–6)
More humor and challenge can be enjoyed by the young child in
reading and participating in this second fun-packed book of puzzles, jokes, riddles, and rhymes.

Withers, Carl, ed.   *Favorite Rhymes from A Rocket in My Pocket*
                    Scholastic, 50¢   (K–3)
Sixty-six traditional chanting rhymes and jingles from all sections
of the United States. It's the type of material children very young
request.

ADULT GUIDES

DUFF, ANNIS   *Bequest of Wings: A Family's Pleasures with Books*
Viking, $1.45

This book contains the "intimate reading experiences shared by two children and their parents." To be used by teacher and librarians with children.

SAWYER, RUTH   *The Way of the Storyteller*
Viking, $1.65

Describes the origins of storytelling as a folk art rooted in the past experiences of a people. Included here for the teacher's reference and useful to the librarian for improving the skill of storytelling.

SAYERS, FRANCES CLAREK   *Summoned by Books: Essays and Speeches*
Viking, $1.35

This is an informative book about books and reading by a leading authority in her field. It will be valuable for the reference collection and for the teacher and librarian.

DIRECTORY OF PUBLISHERS

ABINGDON	Abingdon Press, 201 Eighth Ave. S., Nashville, Tenn. 37202
ACROPOLIS	Acropolis Books, Colortone Bldg., 2400 17th St., N.W., Washington, D.C. 20099
AIRMONT	Airmont Publishing Co., Inc., 22 East 60th St., New York 10022
ASSOCIATION	Association Press, 291 Broadway, New York 10007
AVON	Avon Books, 959 Eighth Ave., New York 10019
BANTAM	Bantam Books, Inc., 666 Fifth Ave., New York 10019
BEACON	Beacon Press, 25 Beacon St., Boston, Mass. 02108
BERKLEY	Berkley Publishing Corporation, 200 Madison Ave., New York 10016
DELL	Dell Publishing Co., Inc. 750 Third Ave., New York 10017
DOVER	Dover Publications, Inc., 180 Varick St., New York 10014
DUTTON	E. P. Dutton & Co., Inc., 201 Park Ave. S., New York 10003
FRIENDSHIP	Friendship Press, 475 Riverside Dr., New York 10027
GOLDEN	Golden Books, Western Publishing Company, Inc., 850 Third Ave., New York 10022
GROSSET	Grosset & Dunlap, Inc., 51 Madison Ave., New York 10010

Harcourt	Harcourt Brace Javanovich, Inc., 757 Third Ave., New York 10017
Harper	Harper & Row, Publishers, 10 East 53rd St., New York 10022
Lancer	Lancer Books, Inc., 1560 Broadway, New York 10036
Macmillan	The Macmillan Company, 866 Third Ave., New York 10022
NAL	New American Library Inc., 1301 Ave. of the Americas, New York 10019
Penguin	Penguin Books Inc., 7110 Ambassador Rd., Baltimore, Md. 21207
Pocket	Pocket Books, 1 West 39th St., New York 10018
Popular	Popular Library, Inc., 355 Lexington Ave., New York 10017
Pyramid	Pyramid Publications, 444 Madison Ave., New York 10022
Rand	Rand McNally & Co., Box 7600, Chicago, Ill. 60680
St. Martin's	St. Martin's Press, Inc., 175 Fifth Ave., New York 10010
Schocken	Schocken Books, Inc., 67 Park Ave., New York 10016
Scholastic	Scholastic Book Services, 50 West 44th St., New York 10036 (With the exception of Starline books, Scholastic titles should be ordered directly from the publisher.)
Scribner	Charles Scribner's Sons, 597 Fifth Ave., New York 10017
Union	Union of American Hebrew Congregations, 838 Fifth Ave., New York 10021
Viking	The Viking Press, Inc., 625 Madison Ave., New York 10022
WSP	Washington Square Press, 630 Fifth Ave., New York 10020
Wonder	Wonder-Treasure Books, 51 Madison Ave., New York 10010
Young Readers	Young Readers Press, Inc., 1120 Ave. of the Americas, New York 10036

AUTHOR INDEX

TITLE INDEX